My Yoga of Expression

Books by Karnamrita Das

Give to Live

With the North American Grihastha (Family) Vision Team:
Heart and Soul Connections:
A Devotional Guide to Marriage, Service, and Love

The Phoenix Rises out of the "Yoga of Despair:"
Collected Free Verse Poems Vol. 2

Karnamrita Das

My Yoga of Expression

Collected Free Verse Poems Vol. 1

I shall pass this way but once; any good that I can do or any kindness I can show to any human being, let me do it now. Let me not defer nor neglect it, for I shall not pass this way again.
Etienne de Grellet, Quaker Missionary

Copyright @ 2016 Karnamrita Das
All rights reserved.
Published in the United States by Inword Publishers.
ISBN 978-0-9969156-2-5
Cover and text design by Inword Publishers

*This book is dedicated to those of you who
feel challenged by an existential crisis as you try
to make sense of your life and this often crazy world;
to all sincere seekers of divine wisdom and lasting love;
to those of you who are engaged in yoga or spiritual practice;
and to my brothers and sisters in Bhakti who are looking
for ways to stay the course of lifelong devotional practice.
May you all be blessed to find answers and light to
direct you toward your most cherished
ideals and goals.*

MY GRATITUDE   X

INVOCATION   XII

PREFACE: Introduction to Completion:
Where and When Does a Circle/Cycle Begin?   xv

FOREWORD   XXI

1 MEANING AND PURPOSE THROUGH POEMS   1
   My Yoga of Poetry   2
   Dead Poet's Society   4
   Lessons from Temple Service, Writing, and Snow   6
   True Eloquence   10
   My Sacred Duty and Offering—
      to Krishna and to You   12
   On the Path of Perfection—We Keep On, Keepin' On   16
   The Creative Process Is a Gracious Gift   19
   The Life of the Poem, or Forgetting the Soul?   21

2 THE NATURAL WORLD   27
   Reflections in the Woodshed   28
   Ordinary, Everyday Mystic   32
   The Fall Wind's Message   35
   Is Yard Work Devotional Service?   41
   Before Enlightenment, Stacking Wood   44
   The Flower's Smile   46
   Amidst Lush Nature's Beauty   48
   Listening for Spring   52
   External, Internal Seasons   54

The Rama Green of Spring Inspires   57
On Meeting Life with a Smile and Spiritual Eyes,
   Wide Awake   59
The Joy of Rain   62
Listen to the Earth: Be a Giver   64
Appreciating the Blessings of Nature   67
Receiving Nature's Aesthetic Wisdom   70

3 RELATIONSHIPS   75

Fool for Love   76
As Relationships Change, So Must We   77
Dreaming a Quest Up the Relationship Mountain   81
Relationships Are Everything   87
Failure Is the Pillar of Success—
   After Slipping, Again, Rise Up!   90
The Interior Castle; Saved from Quicksand   94
The Holy Grail of Relationships   96
Relationships, Togetherness   99
Painful Impetus for Spiritual Practice: Good Grief!   101
The Power of Grace in Meeting Our Guru   103

4 SPIRITUAL PERSPECTIVES   107

Classroom of Life 101   108
Is Life or Am I, Complex or Simple?   110
Beyond the Land of Death and Doubt—
   The Homeland of the Heart, Vrindavan   113
Lord Chaitanya's Moon of the Holy Name Still Rises   116
Beyond the Influence of the Stars   120
The Spiritual Basics Must Be Mastered
   (And It Takes a Long Time!)   124
Prabhupada's Arrival in America   126

Ring Around the Rosie: We All Fall Down/Rise Up   128
Spiritual Variety in Universal Oneness   131
Impurely Imitating, but Eventually Waking Up   134
Simple, Profound Truth   135

5 LIVING FULLY   139
Becoming More by Working at Kindred Spirits   140
My Life's Creed   141
Divine Change Agent   145
On Preparing for Death While Living Fully   148
To Begin Coming to Krishna:
   How Much Faith Is Enough?   151
Living and Dying for Krishna:
   Emperor Parikchit's Example   156
What Is Life About? Where Is Happiness?   159
Neither Here Nor There—So, Where Are You?   162
Saved from Cosmic Crud   164
The Day the Sun Didn't Rise   165
Deck-Mates—Tiny Construction Instruments
   Try to Remember Krishna   169
A Lotus in the Redwoods   171

APPENDICES   175
GLOSSARY   177
EPILOGUE   193
ABOUT THE ARTIST   197
ABOUT THE AUTHOR   198
PRAYER   203
FACING DEATH TO LIVE MORE FULLY   207
I AM DYING! WHY IS THERE DEATH?   209
CANCER BRINGS THE SEEDS OF CHANGE   212

MY GRATITUDE

This is the "Acknowledgements" section, but that didn't seem a strong enough term to express my appreciation for all those involved in the creation of this book. Another reason I wanted to call this section, "My Gratitude," is that growing up, gratitude wasn't in my vocabulary. While I now know the importance of gratitude for living a happy and meaningful life, it has only been during the last ten years that gratitude has been a regular practice for me. Presently, I endeavor to see the universe as friendly and God as my dear-most friend and well-wisher. Thus, whatever happens in my life is meant for my highest good, even cancer.

The cancer cells in my body have provided a fire to motivate my progress in publishing this book, and so I must express my gratitude to them, even as I do my best to bid them adieu. While any disease has multiple factors in its cause and in the lessons it is meant to teach—physical, psychological, and spiritual—my most important analysis is this: since this disease has been a tremendous wake-up call for me in my spiritual practices and has motivated me to serve according to what I am inspired to do, I ultimately have to thank the infinite God, whom I know as Krishna, for not giving up on me and for knowing how to motivate me to fulfill my mission.

Though I would have preferred that he would not have needed to employ the cosmic two-by-four to get my attention (ouch!), I will take what I can get. We can judge its effectiveness by the results. I also thank the Lords of my heart and my seen and unseen guides who have given me the inspiration to write and the vision to combine my words into this and other books. Writing has been, and continues to be, a great boon in my life. It has enabled me to express my heart and mind in the service of our souls' awakening. This attempt has helped me more than I can express. As we give, so we receive, with interest compounded!

Many thanks go to Pranada dasi for embarking on the journey of creating Inword Publishers, and for assembling the impressive team who have combined together to create this book. My sincere appreciation goes to Krisangi and her husband Kamalaksa for designing the cover and doing the book's layout; to Ananda-mayi for editing and offering suggestions for the poems; to Nama-dharma for his thoughtful and generous Foreword; to the many persons who read the book in part or in its entirety for giving their valuable impressions; and to you, the current readers, for giving the book its ultimate purpose as an offering from my heart to yours. Thank you all!

INVOCATION

The self-made man or women is really a myth since we are all indebted to those who have gone before us. We have shared their successes or failures, used their strategies in our chosen field, or in a more general way, benefited from inheriting their life skills. Robert Frost's famous poem, "The Road Not Taken," reminds me of a number of pivotal times in my life when I took the road less traveled, such as beginning my spiritual search; taking up Bhakti; pursuing a relationship with my wife; and currently, speaking, teaching, and writing my truth, sharing what resonates with me and what I feel will be helpful to everyone. We all have a mission or calling in life. Our challenge is to discover and accept it, and follow it in faith. We become more by pursuing it, or we risk feeling incomplete and conflicted if we neglect it, both in life and at death.

Two roads diverged in a yellow wood,
And sorry I could not travel both
And be one traveler, long I stood
And looked down one as far as I could
To where it bent in the undergrowth;

Then took the other, as just as fair,
And having perhaps the better claim,
Because it was grassy and wanted wear;

Though as for that the passing there
Had worn them really about the same,

And both that morning equally lay
In leaves no step had trodden black.
Oh, I kept the first for another day!
Yet knowing how way leads on to way,
I doubted if I should ever come back.

I shall be telling this with a sigh
Somewhere ages and ages hence:
Two roads diverged in a wood, and I—
I took the one less traveled by,
And that has made all the difference.

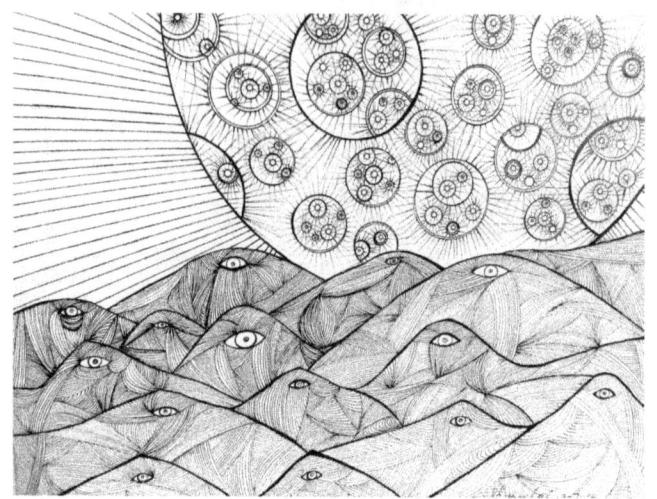

Preface

INTRODUCTION TO COMPLETION
—WHERE AND WHEN DOES A CIRCLE/CYCLE BEGIN?

Every time I write about writing, I think of adding, "Although I have already written too much about writing . . ." Yet today, I have a different angle of vision. It is natural to speak about that with which we are preoccupied. Can I write too much about life, death, or spiritual practice? I think not, and still, I feel somewhat apologetic for writing so much about writing. Whatever my writing is—good, bad, or mediocre—I write about topics that capture my interest and attention, topics that inspire me. Or, I write about what I need to write about. I pray my work may be useful to you on your life's journey of awakening.

I have broken off the following poem from a much longer poem that is now in three parts, which perhaps is kinder to you. Or at least, it is more focused (see "The Interior Castle; Saved from Quicksand" in Chapter 3 for the second and third parts).

The blank page beckons;
inspiration's door opens a crack:
Will it open wide or crash shut?
I'm uncertain whether to begin,
so I pray to the Source of all learning and I sense:
Endeavor and grace create possibilities.
Faithful effort always bears fruit.

The poem reveals itself to openness.
He who hesitates loses inspiration;
the flame only illuminates the moving pen.
God's grace is everywhere, all-pervading.
We create darkness (writer's block) by believing in it.
Nothing is accomplished without faithful endeavor.
Going forward in humble confidence,
I know the result already exists
if the instrument is ready and willing.

A thousand duties compete to distract me,
pulling me in all directions except writing.
Every completion needs a beginning.
Walking past doubt on the road of service,
churning the supplied ingredients,
giving time, heart, and receptivity,
alternating steps with quiet inner listening,
the mountaintop is reached in its own time.

When I think of what I hope to accomplish by writing, I look at what I pray for everyday. Many times a day I pray that I will be empowered to speak, teach, write, and offer healing in a way that is encouraging to my fellow Gaudiya Vaishnavas, as well as to spiritual seekers and people in general. I pray to give them—and you—hope in what's possible, in the process of spiritual practice and attainment, in their (your) own divine potential. I pray to convey the sense that by serving and trying to love God, there is only gain.

Please endeavor to feel the spirit behind my words, especially if some of them are unfamiliar to you. We can connect on many levels: by our condition as fellow humans living at this time, by our desire to improve our lives, by our shared experiences, and by the desire to understand ourselves spiritually. I ask you to take a chance and open your heart in reading. I am doing my best to put everything I am into my writing, and I wish you only the best in every aspect of your life.

I call God Krishna. I see "God" as a title, whereas his name, Krishna, indicates his particular features, his all-attractive, irresistible, human-like appearance. God is Krishna when he wants to take off his crown, so to speak. Krishna wants to be able to share and give love in a way that we, and he, can appreciate. I accept Krishna as the most intimate and original form of God; however, I see that Krishna includes all other forms of God, as in a general sense God is one. While I understand this is a broad view, it is my bias. No one can live without bias, regardless of what we may say or write to the contrary.

Life is short, but it's long enough that we can discover our purpose. In my tradition, our purpose is to make progress in loving and serving Krishna and his devotees. It doesn't matter what one's position is or how disqualified or lacking one may feel—none of that matters. We only have to do our best in our spiritual endeavors. For me, spiritual practice involves chanting the holy name, creating good association, sharing Krishna—or spiritual—consciousness, and offering my life—my home, time, and family—to God, all the while knowing that practice makes perfect.

My hope and prayer is that whoever reads what I write will be inspired on their spiritual path—whatever that may be—and that their inspiration will help those they may touch in turn. I pray that what I write will help others to see their life as purposeful, meant to foster their highest good. The more people who live in this way, practicing kindness and dealing lovingly with the soul and the Divine, the more people will be helped and the better world we will create—one person at a time.

We all need help, and one way to be helped is to help others. Ideally we will reach out to others with a spiritual focus, but any way that we can make a difference matters. In order to grow spiritually, we are assisted by a healthy body and mind. So, I favor spiritual practices that incorporate personal growth work and actions for physical health. This has never seemed more important to me than it does today as I face my possible demise—physically speaking, since there is no death for the soul—through cancer.

"For the soul there is neither birth nor death at any time.
He has not come into being, does not come into being, and
will not come into being. He is unborn, eternal, ever-existing,
and primeval. He is not slain when the body is slain."
(Bhagavad Gita, 2.20)

"As a person puts on new garments, giving up old ones,
the soul similarly accepts new material bodies, giving up
the old and useless ones."
(Bhagavad Gita, 2.22)

"One who has taken his birth is sure to die, and after death
one is sure to take birth again. Therefore, in the unavoidable
discharge of your duty, you should not lament."
(Bhagavad Gita, 2.27)

For years I have wanted to teach what I know and feel, but for various reasons and plausible excuses, and because of my tendency to procrastinate, I have not. Now my cancer diagnosis has changed everything. Now I am living in order to share whatever gifts and wisdom I have been blessed with. To a large extent, this book and my new direction of speaking about how facing death can help us live more fully today can be explained by the spirit of this quote from W. H. Murray:

"Until one is committed, there is hesitancy, the chance to draw back, always ineffectiveness. Concerning all acts of initiative (and creation), there is one elementary truth, the ignorance of which kills countless ideas and splendid plans: that the moment one definitely commits oneself, then Providence moves too. All sorts of things occur to help one that would never otherwise have occurred. A whole stream of events issues from the decision, raising in one's favor all manner of unforeseen incidents and meetings and material assistance, which no man could have dreamt would have come his way. I learned a deep respect for one of Goethe's couplets:

Whatever you can do or dream you can, begin it.
Boldness has genius, power and magic in it!"

Foreword

When Karnamrita dasa first approached me to write a foreword to this collection of poems, I felt honored and humbled. His writings and blog posts on spiritual practice have inspired me for years and have informed how I approach teaching Bhakti to yoga teachers and students alike. He has mentored me, offered me encouragement, served as an example of lifelong commitment to spiritual practice, and helped me navigate through a particularly long-running stretch of writer's block. It is here, then, that I humbly ask for guidance from my guru, in introducing Karnamrita's work, which has supported my spiritual growth and facilitated my work of beginning to recognize that there is beauty in everything, even our greatest challenges.

The notable acharya Swami B. R. Shridhar Maharaja once stated, "the innermost hankering of every living soul is for beauty, love, affection, and harmony."[1] The yearning for this type of connection motivates many, if not all, of our activities throughout our daily lives. When the experience of love captures our heart, we naturally start to share this with others. At times, this sharing happens inadvertently, as is the case when an individual glows from being in love. Other times, it is expressed more intentionally in conversations with friends or through art forms such as song, dance, and, as is this case in this instance, poetry.

---

[1] B. R. Shridhara Maharaja, Loving Search for the Lost Servant (San Jose: Guardian of Devotion Press, 1987), 66.

The verses Karnamrita dasa so generously shares in this collection offer a glimpse into a spiritual practitioner's heart, along with the wisdom that comes from a lifetime dedicated to service and love of God. Karnamrita's poems offer insight into the world of a Bhakta, one who practices Bhakti Yoga, where unmotivated love of God is the ideal. Through his meditations on the natural world, interpersonal relationships, and the interplay of life and death, he presents a fine example of how spiritual practice and learning to love can be a part of our day-to-day activities. As Karnamrita writes, "Everything can teach us / if we are aware."

Throughout the course of this compilation, Karnamrita writes about his relationship with the Divine, which, as a Gaudiya Vaisnava, he refers to as Krishna. Within the mysticism of India, Krishna is often referred to as the personification of love. Gaudiya Vaisnavas perhaps take it one step further, seeing him as Rasaraja, the source of all loving sentiments. Although Karnamrita has this spiritual bias, his poems remain inspiring and accessible for all spiritual seekers regardless of their individual path. In addition to sharing the full spectrum of his love of God, his writing illustrates how one might stay immersed in spiritual pursuits, despite the trials and tribulations of the material world. Karnamrita's courage to share his own process of facing a life-threatening illness clearly demonstrates that our own biggest challenges can be opportunities for deep spiritual growth and personal healing.

The Chandogya Upanishad states, "A person is what his or her deep desire is."[2] From this vantage point, Karnamrita is well

---

[2] Eknath Easwaran, The Upanishads (Canada: The Blue Mountain Center of Meditation, 2007), 126.

situated in this life and beyond, as he seeks only to be a devoted servant of God and to use the time he has with us to inspire others to pursue their heart's deepest longing. Indeed, pursuing meaningful connection and engaging in spiritual practice, as Karnamrita demonstrates throughout his writings, is a boon to all. When we engage life through the lens of a spiritual practitioner, not only do we elevate our own consciousness, we then serve as a beacon for others who are searching for connection to their own truth and heart's desire.

Matt Nelson (Nama-dharma dasa) is a yoga teacher and practitioner who resides in Portland, OR and leads classes, retreats, and continuing education workshops for yoga teachers. His spiritual inquiry began with Chi Gung in 1995 and transitioned to yoga in 2003. Since then, he has had guidance and inspiration from numerous spiritual seekers, with the most notable being Zhander Remete, Peter Sterios, Amy Matthews, and his beloved guru Swami B. V. Tripurari. Matt's classes integrate the heart of Bhakti throughout his fluid approach to Hatha Yoga. He believes in providing joyful, nurturing, structurally sound classes that nourish the soul, support inner-growth, and present a physical challenge appropriately suited for each practitioner. To find out more about Matt, visit his website: mattnelsonyoga.com

Chapter 1

MEANING AND PURPOSE
THROUGH MY POEMS

The opposite of my intent for writing poems is expressed by the contemporary poet, Dean Young, who said, "I'm much more interested in a poem you can never "get" than the poem you can get after reading it once."[3] To me, the purpose of writing is to communicate meaning. If I fail to do this, I fail. While I appreciate creative expression, I don't feel it has value for its own sake. It must convey meaning. I hope my poetry provides food for thought and contemplation about life and the larger world, as well as "The Most High," our Source, the Supreme Spirit, God, or whatever name you may give to our Higher Power that sustains the universe and our very selves.

---

[3] Young, Dean. "Imagination at the Center: A Profile of Dean Young." By Kevin Nance. Poets & Writers, September/October 2015.

My Yoga of Poetry

Wanting to frame my expression
in contemporary, though ancient words—
would it be vainglory
to call my "personal" ramblings
a "yoga" of poetic expression?
By this, I don't mean flawless.
I mean I write in the spirit
to obtain union with God
by whatever means I have.

As many people know,
"yoga" and "yoke" have similar meanings:
as a yoke links an animal to a cart,
so yoga connects our heart to Divinity.
This is the meaning of the phrase
"yoga of anything:" all things can be used
to join our actions or thoughts to the Supreme.
This is the intention of my "poems."

Calling my poems "yoga"
doesn't proclaim their eloquence
or imply my "style" is perfect,
but it highlights a spiritual purpose:
I write as a devotional offering,
to be enthused and to enthuse others,
to share Bhakti Yoga philosophy,
to document my service aspirations,
all the while praying

to infuse everything I do with love,
to see challenges as spiritual opportunities.

I even hesitate to call my words "poetry,"
nor would my very poetic friends,
expert in meter, rhyme, and metaphor.
I was never trained in the craft.
I likely break all the rules —
yet it works for me as a kind of shorthand
to tell what moves me or what's happening around me.
It helps me to focus and condense my thoughts
with the prayer that we will all benefit.

So please, call it what you will —
free verse or prose poetry,
ramblings of a mad Bhakta,
or simply creative expression.
Regardless, I hope my effort
inspires you to take up the holy name
and to take up spiritual practices realistically,
(or try them on for size!)
sustainably, in good and difficult times.
I hope to foster real and honest introspection,
to help you progress through spiritual yoga stages
always keeping the goal in mind —
we will become our highest ideal!

Dead Poet's Society

Some modern poetry leaves me cold
(though the poet's allure is appealing).
I rarely find meaningful work
of consequence to my life,
either emotionally or spiritually,
which to me is all-important.

Why should I have to work so hard
to unravel the meaning of a poem,
like a detective searching for a clue?
I find myself shifting through
reams of so-called evidence,
finding a children's playground
of no consequence.

It may sound terribly proud
to discount a poet's sincere effort,
yet we all have our lens
through which we determine value or its lack
with only so much time to invest.

For my heart's expression, I write
my life's struggles, aspirations, and joys.
I glorify God and his devout, the path
of spiritual attainment, *Vedic* scriptures,
and Self-realization—the soul's hankerings.

Just as I have no time for poems
in which I can't find substantial, relevant meaning,

some readers will have no time for my poems
that mention God—what to speak of Krishna,
devotion, surrender, and mysticism.
Regardless, I can only write what moves me.

(Though I may miss the mark myself)
To me, good poetry is this:
that which pulls me in, makes me curious,
grasps my attention, touches my heart,
allows me to enter the world of the poet,
shows me a different angle, a new perspective, a shared, *Aha*!

Should I hide my writing in religious journals,
rarely to be read, spoken about, or contemplated?
Or is it acceptable—in a time when anything goes—
to have no interest in expression for expression's sake?
A world without meaning and purpose
is like an empty rice husk or a computer with no CPU.

Of course, on a human level,
I respect all authentic expression of feelings.
This is not a soapbox to decry modern life,
just my thirst for meaning and spiritual purpose
in life, work, family, art, conversation, and expression.

With 65 years behind me, my body's temporariness
increasingly confirms the *Gita's* view of the body and soul:
though I pray to make my last years the best,
no life's duration is guaranteed.
Any breath or heartbeat may be the last.

Four decades of spiritual practice will bear fruit—
my mind fixed on transcendence.
My realized determination arises from this knowledge:
the world's value is in that which facilitates the soul's urge
to be freed from bondage, to return to God's love.
(When will that day be mine?)

Thus I write verse for that purpose:
to find the utility of matter for spiritual practice,
accepting the necessity of work, growth, family, and healing
with the adage, *the way out is through*,
always keeping my spiritual goal to guide and inform me.

Lessons from Temple Service, Writing, and Snow

This poem has been
waiting for weeks—
Oh help me Lord,
will it ever be complete?
Will it adequately convey
what I truly want to say—
a kind of snapshot
of my experience or perception?

Oh the pinching insecurities
of the human, what to speak of
the wonderings of the writer,
asking, *If you could
be behind my eyes for a day,
would compassion or distain
intensely awaken in you?
Would you be moved to love
or shun me forever?
Seeing the heart-flow
of my writings, would you
judge them as valuable
or worse than moldy cabbage?*

But, to the topic at hand:
After the snowstorm, the Arctic wind
comes roaring in, the fallin,' ruslin' leaves
and bowing swaying trees
sound like forcefully magnified ocean waves.

The lights flicker
reminding us of
yesterday's blackout when
we shoved snow into pots
to melt for bathing and drinking,
causing us to appreciate
things we take for granted:
our dependence is absolute.

As I dress in an Indian *dhoti*
in the early dark morning,

adorning my body with clay *tilak*
markings in twelve places,
preparing for temple services,
I fill large pots
for drinking, just in case.
Going outside to start the car
Arctic winds greet
my bare chest
(so my *tilak* will dry).
I notice the temperature
has dropped considerably.

Waking the temple Deities,
we make an offering to God,
then worship—mangal arati—
a service I have offered with devotion
thousands of times
over many, many years.
While guru prayers are sung,
I pray to give my heart
in joyful meditation,
a prayer of glorification,
again, and again, and again.

I think of my *gurus*,
the great previous teachers,
along with Shri Gaura and Nitai.
Before their pictures on the altar,
I offer an article of worship
and bow my head to each,

their saintly examples
beckoning me to sadhana,
to endeavor for love, *prema*:
Oh fallen soul, aspiring Bhakta,
offer your heart in service
while hearing, chanting, and writing
to please Guru and Radha-Krishna.
Give up your reluctance
and lethargy by realizing
your life can become perfect
by blessings from above,
through service to others,
and the Kirtan Avatar.

I return home bathed
from service and now,
in the morning light,
the roaring wind has abated.
I return to chilly stillness,
demonstrating life cycles
of breathing in and out;
of falling snow, then thawing;
of bitter cold, then sweltering heat;
of going forward and coming back;
of taking birth, then dying again—
the circle game repeats.

When oh when will my soul awaken,
through with desires and drama,
to attain shelter—service

to my dear friends
and well-wishers, my beloved
Lords, Radha-Krishna?

True Eloquence

According to Krishnadas Kaviraja
in *Chaitanya Charitamrita*,
Essential truth spoken concisely
is true eloquence.

Unfortunately, brevity
is not one of my stellar qualities.

Some people talk
to hear their own voice;
being full of themselves,
their words feel bloated.

More important than mere words
is the spirit of urgency they convey—
sincerity, love, emotionality, and high purpose
attracts others to their own soul and to God.

Lord Chaitanya played
the role of an ideal teacher,

but wrote only eight verses
and often didn't speak much.

Usually, great Bhakti teachers write
many commentaries or books,
yet Shri Chaitanya taught mostly
through example and through his disciples.

He converted the King's guru,
Sarvabhauma, by remaining silent,
and converted the prominent monist philosopher,
Prakasananda, by showing extraordinary humility.

Head priest, Venkata Bhatta,
was attracted by the Lord's joking,
and many others were attracted
by his ecstatic singing and dancing.

He demonstrated the ideal life
of a God-intoxicated person,
fully absorbed in love for Krishna,
in the mood of Radha's separation.

Those of us who were touched
by Shri Chaitanya's life and teachings,
by the grace of his followers,
try to explain our experience.

This eternal knowledge is passed
down through the generations

as each person who takes it up
presents it according to their realization.

Only those who are empowered
with Krishna's *shakti* can be especially effective
in presenting the essence
of scripture in a way that attracts hearts.

Nevertheless, I keep trying
to share the highest ecstatic truth
according to my limited capacity
because even the attempt purifies.

Every day and every poem is
a new opportunity for purification,
a chance to go deeper into transcendence
by uncovering love for Krishna.

My Sacred Duty and Offering— to Krishna and to You

I'm feeling negligent—
I've been absent from writing,
attending to many services,
pressing demands of time,

unable to think and write—
a most sacred responsibility.

Forgive me for expressing again
my thoughts about my writing service.
It's an important reminder for me
that I have a vital duty to my mentors,
previous teachers, and Shri Chaitanya
to shine a light on Krishna.

My labor of love to them
is expressed in my offering to you:
to those who read this book,
whether out of curiosity about Krishna,
or compelled by an inner, existential crisis,
I offer my expression of how Bhakti lives in me.

Sharing my spiritual life
as I live in the world,
as I experience bliss or difficulty,
I demonstrate that though I'm imperfect,
the life of even a low devotee of Krishna
has meaning and benefit for seekers.

My writing isn't just official philosophy,
dry dogma, or religious formularies.
I don't want to preach "at" you in elitist,
absolutist, either/or terms.
I want to offer you a practical application
of what my heart has become.

Philosophy is only useful
if it's practiced every day,
put to the test in the struggles
we all go through with dismay.
We can find shelter and relief
in applying spiritual ways.

Throughout the so-called ordinary,
we find Krishna's loving hand
if we are trained to look
beyond externals, not labeling
positive or negative ahead of time,
but seeing through optimistic faith.

Everything is about relationships—
philosophy and religion need a face,
otherwise, who will take it up?
Who will see the value if practitioners
are not good people—joyful, peaceful,
spiritually sincere, and purified?

So while you may see
my picture too frequently
in my poems, where I sketch images
of seemingly mundane things
like traveling, visiting parents,
gardening, building, and the like—

the important thing is
the feeling conveyed
of the spiritual current flowing

throughout my being.
The important thing is
that life's divisional boxes
become blurred through Krishna consciousness.

There isn't a box for what's spiritual
and another for what's material.
Perhaps it seems that way at first,
yet gradually we find Krishna
everywhere, in everything
we do, touch, feel, or say.

Even before the perfection of *prema,*
with heart-vision fixed on Krishna,
by doing what fosters Bhakti,
we find our life transformed
by our constant dedication
to our one supreme goal.

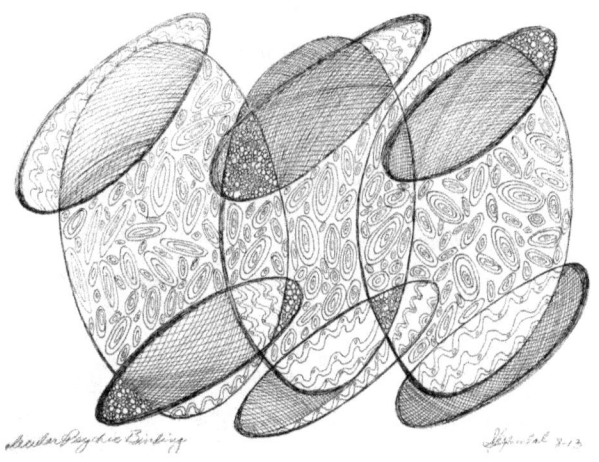

On the Path of Perfection—
We Keep On, Keepin' On

I'm not completely sure what it is
that brings the urge to write and express—
what? The intensity I feel in my heart—
so much more than I could
possibly express—though I try.

In some ways, I'm at peace
in my body, awakening Krishna's
gifts of service, yet part of me
remembers that I'm a soul who
doesn't need a body, and I want out.

I do know I have to remain here
though contrary feelings swirl inside.
Writing helps sort them out,
and I hope to help you know that
you are not alone in duality and struggle.

In the *Gita*, we learn that the world
is constantly changing: different emotions, different seasons
different stages of mind, different ages of the body,
different forms of karma and mercy—up, down, around,
forward, backward—pulled by competing modes,
we're never the doer.

By blessings, spiritual knowledge, experience, and *sadhana*,
we learn that all these changes and dualities

are unnatural for us, the soul, and thus
we seek the true permanence and stability of being
in our constitutional nature—in *Krishna prema* and *seva*.

I know I'm getting somewhere here—
my eyes are tearing up.
It's like I'm getting a glimpse of my
true, authentic Self beyond matter—
consciousness, the experiencer—trying to come out.

Other than uncovering the soul,
there is no other problem (to be realized!).
Because we have desires, we have
created obligations and responsibilities
by which we define ourselves.

Alas, the false ego runs
my life in the vain pursuit
to keep the illusion going. I know I keep
saying this, but have we really understood?
Krishna's the real center; we orbit around him.

The common themes I express
in verse indicate I stand before a vast
chasm and a high hurdle that I must jump beyond,
over, through to the other side of *anarthas*,
to the high stages of devotion, to *prema*.

Like a baby learning to walk
by repeatedly falling, though relentlessly
trying—undaunted by failure,

determined to succeed, knowing we will stand—
we must humbly, yet confidently, approach Krishna.

If we are sincere in our endeavor,
keeping alive the fire of faith,
praying for help to always be steady
in our attempt, our love for Krishna
will be uncovered, and we'll live in his abode.

Then, all parts of us will be
in harmony and unity. We'll be satisfied
in our true, pure nature of total giving
and service to that Person who is more
dear than life. We'll attain ideal, lasting love.

We can't go to Krishna's temple
with our shoes on—we have to leave
our false conceptions, our material dirt and desires
outside, putting on the spiritual raiment
of a pure heart, loving desires, and selfless service.

Our attempts to express our deepest love
and affection for Krishna are never finished. We keep
singing his glories and pastimes forever, continuing
to serve by sharing our love as we desire—
cooking, cleaning, and decorating for him—
now and in perfection.

The Creative Process Is a Gracious Gift

The great Brahma instructs us.
He's celebrated in the *Vedas* as the "Creator,"
though this is only secondarily so.
He's supplied material ingredients
and assembles planets and all bodies
according to internal inspiration,
a subtle seed within.
He gives credit to his Source and Deity.

The building or addition we're constructing
already exists. Similarly, the poem or essay
we labor to produce and perfect
only appears newly manufactured.
We are only instruments of creation.

As the house builds itself,
we don't write the poem.
The poem writes and nurtures us—
as does the blog, painting, sculpture, song, or film—
though this fact doesn't mean
the result is universally appreciated.

So, you are a published author?
The latest literary sensation?
Do your feet no longer touch the ground?
No need to answer nature's call?
Though lavish praise garlands you,
if you don't believe in your soul,
or the source of your inspiration, joy, and peace,

then all appreciation is shallow
and the world is empty and void.

Are we great
because of the world's opinion?
Or are we great
due to who we *are*: the *quality* of our life,
our intentions for writing,
our reasons for living and endeavoring?

Though those attached to matter will not agree,
spiritual seekers are at peace
with their embodiment, taking pleasure in their soul,
perceiving material life like the flapping of a fish
on land or like the fate of the sandcastle on the beach.

On death row,
we only have so many meals,
heartbeats, breaths, and excretions.
But that doesn't mean life isn't an opportunity—
it is (if kept in perspective)!
Life only has meaning due to the life force.
Consciousness comes from the soul,
which is far greater than matter,
and the Supreme Soul is infinitely grander still.

Even after driving 1,000 miles
without steering, we fall into the ditch.
Past accolades cannot sustain us.
We are defined moment by moment—
regardless of our achievements,

bank balance, possessions, or home.
More important than these externals
is the person we have become
in the process of collecting them.

The Life of the Poem, or Forgetting the Soul?

Sitting before Their Metamorphoses,
our newly painted, revitalized Radha-Krishna Deities—
living art infused with Bhakti—we sense
indescribably, yet noticeably, increased beauty.
Chanting the king of poetry, the *Gayatri mantra*,
my heart bubbles up with the desire to share.
I'm provided cream and milk
from which I make butter and ghee, and offer it.

The steamroller of time moves along,
pulling all into its circle of limitations.
So we try to accomplish something of value
before our day, or life, is flattened and changed.
We don't want to be caught up in merely existing for naught.
We want to slow down to learn soul lessons—
accepting help and helping others
with thoughtful words, verses for Krishna.

Is something art or poetry
just because I or someone else says so?

What about one who throws garbage
on a canvas and tells us we should know,
This is profound truth and glorious art?
Or what about rhapsodic rhythms, profound metaphors,
and brilliantly ornate word arrangements
that only titillate the mind, not the soul?

While I appreciate and aspire to learn
the writer's or poet's craft in displaying
literary embellishments and insightful metaphors,
in crafting great stories and interesting, stimulating reads—
art for art's sake misses life's real point.
It's a jugglery of vocabulary without purpose.
It's merely arrogance if we forget our Source
of inspiration and life, the giver of our abilities.

For example: A fourteen-line poem is examined
and lavishly praised by teacher and students
who find layers of meaning in metaphors.
They're amazed at its complexity in simplicity and conclude
the author didn't make it directly,
but connected to their unconscious mind.
Truth is revealed by imagination and intellect,
which by omission are their gods to praise.

Everyone has a lens or bias
through which thoughts are filtered, so I will be criticized
as a shallow theist who is against modern art and creativity.
But no—we should use every tool available,
both modern and ancient art forms,

not for nothing except human vainglory,
but rather, as an expression of devotion,
soul philosophy, the glory of God.

I don't criticize the writer's gifts
only because mine are truly limited,
smugly saying meaning is everything
while having no poetic sensibilities.
Yet for me, the spiritual quest is all-important—
if not meaning, at least the search for it.
I use words as a bridge to revelation,
a blessing bestowed to uncover God.

The rising sun heralds the new day of possibilities.
It's the Lord's watchful eye, a cosmic time machine.
Indoor plants seem to grow for themselves,
yet are benefited by beautifying our temple.
Everything teaches us about the Unseen,
the sustaining, nurturing Force, Shri Krishna,
whom we are meant to know, love, and serve.
He gives us life, inspiration, and words for our poems.

The purpose of life is a life of purpose.
Robert Byrne

The purpose of life is not to be happy. It is to be useful, to be honorable, to be compassionate, to have it make some difference that you have lived and lived well.
Ralph Waldo Emerson

The mystery of human existence lies not in just staying alive, but in finding something to live for.
Fyodor Dostoyevsky, The Brothers Karamazov

It is not that we have so little time but that we lose so much. . . . The life we receive is not short but we make it so; we are not ill provided but use what we have wastefully.
Seneca, On the Shortness of Life

One should learn how to dovetail everything in the service of the Lord, for everything is connected to Krishna. That is the real purpose of life and secret of success.

Although the purpose of life is to become spiritually rich, unfortunate men, misguided as they are, are always engaged in trying to become materially rich.
Shrila Prabhupada, from explanations of two verses in the Vedic text, Shrimad Bhagavatam, 4th and 7th Cantos respectively

Chapter 2

THE NATURAL WORLD

Krishna continued: I am the taste of water, the light of the sun and the moon, the syllable Om in the Vedic mantras; I am the sound in ether and ability in man. / I am the original fragrance of the earth, and I am the heat in fire. I am the life of all that lives, and I am the penances of all ascetics. / Know that I am the original seed of all existences, the intelligence of the intelligent, and the prowess of everyone who is powerful. / I am the strength of the strong, devoid of passion and desire. I am sex life which is not contrary to religious principles.

Bhagavad Gita, 7:8–11

Reflections in the Woodshed

I.
Wandering into the woodshed,
scratching my head,
a roof with four air sides,
mostly dry wood mixed
with sprinkled melting snow.

Meditating on experience,
wondering how to convey it
meaningfully—does it matter?
Well, it does to me.
Otherwise, why write?

In a perfect world,
my desire to express
or share who I am
and aspire to be
would match your necessity.

Even if only a few read this,
I pray my effort—offering
my life to Krishna, detached
from results—is useful
in helping them spiritually.

My winter life includes
frequent woodpile visits.
These days, that's my only contact

with the "raw" earth.
I stay inside every day.

Not the "wilderness"
by any means, yet compared to
the city, some might label it so:
our home on four acres,
similar *Vaishnava* neighbors.

II.
Interesting times of snow:
last week a foot,
this morning six inches,
now rain and mixed wet stuff.
I'm grateful for boots and warmth.

I'm telling you this
to share my joy of simplicity,
sitting on damp wood listening
to a cacophony—water symphony—
with no rush or place to go.

Melting snow crashes down,
raindrops crackle on plastic,
on the tin roof, and spill from gutters.
My face is chilled, refreshed—
"Life 101:" lessons for peace.

Huge buzzards have a home
in our trees—sometimes over a hundred—

though today only a few glide overhead,
despite freezing rain.
They're unmoved by such weather.

Can any high-tech gadget
compare or compete with this?
And then, add thoughts of
Krishna's display of energy and power—I smile,
revering a life of goodness, simplicity.

Oh, the irony of my writing—
lowly, juvenile, inadequate—
its first birth on the Net
enables my criticism of technology
while I'm dependent on it!

If we really have some experience
of Krishna in our lives,
then truly, *It's all good*.
Even calamities benefit us
with potential service.

Imperfect? It certainly is.
But we are, by our guru's grace,
engaging in Bhakti Yoga,
removing lifetimes of ignorance
and divinely reorienting our Self.

III.
Are the mist drops
a problem for the page?

Or do I just move over,
happy with another stanza?
Do we change or adapt?

The world's full
of invented "wheels"
we can easily use to accomplish
our necessities, to live a balanced,
peaceful life focused on the soul's interest.

We give to our families,
to ourselves, to devotees,
and to temples. We work,
trying to offer the objects
of our affection to the Lord of our heart.

One of my devotional mottos:
Give this one life to Krishna,
though it's short and fast.
Use your desires for him,
develop a serving ego,
and share this path with others.

It's all a matter of consciousness—
our faith and intentions,
looking for Krishna's hand,
using ours to serve his,
thinking, *What can I give?*

Do what you have to, yet
figure out a way

to connect it to Krishna.
Be kind, listen, share your heart,
chant his name, and read his word.

Be peaceful and satisfied,
yet not complacent.
Keep good company.
Stretch yourself spiritually,
fixed on the goal of *prema*.

Everyone's life is important,
though utilization determines success.
Material purposes are of relative value
since we're souls, part of God.
Realizing this truth is of lasting benefit.

Ordinary, Everyday Mystic

Change is a constant, ordinary
in nature. Slow and steady,
it's obscured by our mind's absorption
till a critical mass, *Aha!* moment.

Walking outside to the mailbox,
I'm greeted by fall's embrace.

Colored leaves fall and swirl,
gracefully decorating the ground.

And my special love, the wind,
sways the trees by its force,
creating the soothing, swishing sound
that races by my ears as I breathe it in.

Never-boring sights and sounds—
objectively, it's "predictable" fall weather,
but in my subjective experience I'm exhilarated,
joyfully touched amidst aesthetic beauty.

Though fall weather is "expected,"
nothing is remotely ordinary:
many shades and nuances of colors,
flowers that bloom before the frost.

Behind the dancing, singing trees,
incredible blue sky is painted
by moving, multi-colored clouds.
If this is ordinary, there're no words for extraordinary!

Yet, a peaceful, satisfied mind is required
to observe and really appreciate simplicity.
We must live joyfully with spiritual practice
instead of being mad for external happiness.

We can transform "ordinary" into super-amazing
by bringing artistic beauty, the Source—Krishna—
into our lives, not just intellectually, but

lovingly, honestly attempting to give our heart and soul.

Until we realize our Self to be a lover of God,
we must endeavor to bring Krishna into every moment,
uncovering him in the smallest and the greatest—
in wind, rain, and drought; in seasons, and in birth and death.

Let's arise from the dream without
identifying our soul with fleeting matter,
without struggling to exist and to avoid death,
thinking the universe empty and without purpose.

Firmly embracing Bhakti we find
everything is favorable for service.
The world becomes the abode of joy.
Even sorrow or calamity are Krishna's embrace!

Loving Krishna becomes our magnificent obsession,
and life revolves around our heart's aspiration.
Spiritual practice gives us pleasure and satisfaction,
our everyday life transformed by mystical vibration.

The Fall Wind's Message

Sitting in my chair
for forest meditation,
chanting *japa*,
Oh Radhe, Oh Krishna!
Please capture me—
my whole mind,
heart, and soul!
End my material existence!
Pull my attention and desires
to you alone! Let me have
no other interests!
Krishna Krishna, Hare Hare

After a few revolutions
of chanting *Hare Krishna*
in the pleasant fall warmth,
I just sit and listen,
asking, *What can I learn?*

The wind answers my inquiry,
gently massaging the trees
with its air current,
speaking the language of the ages.

Everything can teach us
if we are aware,
listening for clues
instead of dreaming idly
of the improvable future

or past, instead of bemoaning
our bad choices or current fate,
instead of lusting for enjoyment.

What could
Krishna's material nature
be saying through
its windy voice?
Ah, the seasons
demonstrate the cycles
of all life, our own included.
Nothing material lasts.
Changes are inevitable.
Everything returns to
its starting point,
over and over,
until it finds
ultimate rest.

Spring gives birth
to the year and all possibilities.
Nature seems to return
to life after a long sleep
and the colors of newness burst forth
in incredible dynamism,
attracting everyone's attention:
there are bright green leaves
and unlimited varieties
of colors in flowers
that gradually turn to seeds
or fruits that ripen

and are harvested in the fall
or drop to the ground,
lying dormant
in the cold, bleak winter,
waiting to awaken again
next year . . .

When will we return
to the land of no return
where all things are possible,
where everything dances together
in total harmony,
centered on the love
of everyone's heart?
When will we be free
from birth, disease,
old age, and death?
When will we live
in unlimited, blissful love
in relationship with
the Perfect Person and
those who love him most?

Throughout the day
the leaves are falling—
then, with the wind
swooshing everywhere they
finally stop softly dropping,
going up and around
like so many kites or free agents,
or they circle around me—

surround sound—
like the "will-o'-the-wisp."

There is no sound
in nature as beautiful
to me as the rush
of the wind in the trees—
the invisible moving the seen,
the power of God touching us.

I do my best to take the sound
in through my two tiny ear holes.
As the winds speed up or slow,
the trees dance in time, swaying
back and forth,
mixing different temps
of warm and cool air
with the smell of moist
leaves on the forest floor,
damp from recent rain.
In the distance—
the sound of thunder,
the sight of both white puffy and rain
clouds bringing uncertainty
of what will come.

Nature celebrates life,
indirectly pointing to
the Creator or Source—
for me, Shri Krishna.
Though we can do our best

to directly glorify him and sense him
everywhere—in scenic nature
or at work or school—
he's the sustainer,
maintainer, creator, destroyer,
and so much more.
He's our dearmost friend
and ultimate love.

We can imagine how wonderful
and beautiful he is,
the background and source
of nature—*his* nature.
So even I, a tiny covered soul,
can appreciate to some extent
the attractiveness, wonder, and beauty
of Krishna's Material Energy—
splendid and orderly, yet
so varied and unexpected
amidst regular cycles,
never boring or old.
There is certainty within variety.

Though winter is coming,
the attraction of autumn is still uplifting,
spectacular, and refreshing,
as it reveals and reminds us
of our tininess. But it also reminds us
that we have our part to play—
to be good stewards
of the world while we focus

on the Ultimate Reality
(Reality the Most Beautiful).
It reminds us that we are important
to Krishna, who wants
our company and love.

Such an endearing truth:
though he is complete,
Krishna also pines for our love.
And, if we also want
him more than anything,
then we will go
where our heart is focused
by the Law of Necessity.
Devotion is the real secret
of secrets, the inner purpose
of the *Vedas*, uniting us
with Krishna by love!

Is Yard Work Devotional Service?

The "jungle" is returning.
Time to weed whack, to trim,
and to drive the lawn tractor
before it rains again.

I begin trimming under
grey skies, and then it pours.
Putting on a poncho to keep dry,
I weed by hand, listening:

the roar of the rain
in the trees, the swish of wind,

raindrops on my covered head—
I think the *Hare Krishna* mantra.

Pondering in my plastic poncho,
I think about my life as I look at the beautiful,
verdant forest, intensely green grass,
and colorful flowers—yellows and reds.

Is my yard work devotional service
just because I think I'm a devotee?
Have I offered the weeding to Krishna,
thinking our home and yard his?

Certainly I believe in theory,
and I follow the guidelines,
but what do I really feel?
After all, my heart is where I live.

I act dutifully, often in prayer, yet
if I really knew my house is Krishna's
home, I would keep it much cleaner,
and the yard better maintained!

Trying to be more self-reliant
while consuming less energy,
my son installed solar water collectors
and an "on demand" water heater.

Yet, I think how we live in the US—
with central air conditioning

and all our convenience machines—
would make a Himalayan yogi laugh.

Yet, Bhakti is very generous,
and under a guru's shelter we dovetail
our conditioning, desires, and occupations,
making Krishna's service our focus.

Standard of living is relative.
"Simple living" is an internal evaluation
that varies with person and country.
Who has too much or just enough?

A devotee born rich creates a home
that feels "just" comfortable,
while a devotee born poor
might think that devotee extravagant.

My home could be
a palace in some countries,
yet here it's "middle class,"
and I see it as normal with guest facilities.

Let's adopt what we need to progress
toward our goal of loving and serving Krishna,
whatever allows us to be peaceful
and inspired to serve.

We have to thoughtfully evaluate
whether or not our lifestyle is favorable for service.

We should take care that we're neither
over-endeavoring nor in anxiety about our next meal.

Speaking of which—
now it's time for lunch prasad:
my austere meal of pesto pizza
with artichoke hearts and a salad.
I guess I *am* a yogi after all!

Before Enlightenment, Stacking Wood

Before enlightenment,
stacking wood.
After enlightenment,
stacking wood—with *prema*.

The end of summer can still be hot,
though change is in the air, the secret
whispered by Krishna's nature
through plants and living things.

We try to order wood early
so it can stand and "cure,"
but sometimes our wood guy
brings the wood in slow, country time.

Still, now it's cooler to stack
the wood, and this time my wife
is helping, motivating me,
the procrastinator, to get the job done.

This is the first year
she has helped, and it is much better
than solo. More gets done,
and it's fun!

We chant *Hare Krishna* in our
minds or out loud, discussing God
or a therapy case and joke
that we aren't frontier folk.

We live in the country, but usually
her allergies force her indoors.
Now, though, she's discovered masks,
so she works like a doctor or bandit.

We work for an hour or more
every few days. I bring her
logs, and we both stack.
I go back and forth.

There's the smell of hardwood
and sweat wetting me,
mixing with dirt and coloring
my body and shirt. Both cover my soul.

Evening sun casts a glow
and bugs look for skin.
Spiders and bugs run for cover
as their home is moved.

The earth at our feet—another world
busy with searching and hiding,
victims and victors.
Now we giants disturb both.

Gradually slowing,
my arms and wrists aching—
Ouch! I drop a log on my knee.
Just a bit of pain; the wood tower rises.

We make visible progress, closing one door
to open another, feeling satisfied
with the dignity of simple, outdoor labor
that enables us to lead a life of devotion
(and stay warm this coming winter).

The Flower's Smile

Grey winter skies—
it's frigid wet outside.
Archana sings prayers
and the fire blazes warmth.

Beholding our home Deities—
Radha-Gopinatha—we find shelter
in their uplifting spiritual beauty,
and they kindly glance
to bless everyone.

On the aesthetically-pleasing altar—
Deities galore and glorious,
lovely, jeweled clothing—
the flowers rejoice.

Like trumpets heralding
the sun amidst darkness,
each petal praises God,
arms pointing upward.

The jewels of *Kali*—
simple, yet profound—
it's a joy to behold them,
and I wonder at the Creator.

Our life is a marvel,
with such great opulence,
the wondrous beauty
contrasting with winter's gloom.

The flowers smile—
Radha-Krishna's smile.
We smile and cry,
feeling grateful, blessed.

Returning to timeless *japa*,
hours with my Lords,
by their grace
I gradually wake up.

Amidst Lush Nature's Beauty

I.
A dry day and a half,
ground cracking and thirsty—
there's a forecast of rain,
then clouds joyfully come.

Forest trees
and animals celebrate
the first smell of rain—
then, a delirious downpour.

On the front porch,
I sit to write
in the cool, moist air,
listening, watching, thinking.

Grey skies bring out
the vibrancy of the forest green.
I hear the echo of rain on trees and water
gushes from the gutters.

II.
Whoops! I say, seeing
the empty bird feeder.
The birds sigh
as I fill it with sunflower seeds.

Cute finches and red cardinals,
by virtue of their nature,
teach the truth beyond
superficial appearances:

even though there is plenty,
birds fight for their share,
always afraid, looking around
for possible predators.

Our experience of country life:
it's favorable for spiritual growth
to be thoughtful and observant.
Then, so many lessons are demonstrated.

III.
Contemplating nature's beauty—
it's not independent of God.
We are reminded
to give credit to the Source,
Shri Krishna,
the Cause of all causes.

Amidst lush nature's beauty,
the material law's ugliness:

one creature is food for another.
All struggle against death and disease.
This fact turned Darwin into
an atheist. Why?

Because he didn't know
the beauty of the Creator,
his loving kindness for us
who are part of him
or the perfect purpose behind
what appear to be cruel material laws.

IV.
The world is meant for rectification
through practical education
at the School of Hard Knocks.
The world of death
gives false hopes—
dashed—vain promises,
and illusory, unfulfilled dreams.
The merry-go-round
of birth and death
is meant to push us
to search out our Maker
and his world of blissful light.
There, souls live harmoniously
in unity of godly love and service.

Here, the first sunflowers and zinnias
bloom, finding their place in a vase

before *Radha* and Krishna,
under whose laws
they miraculously grow
from seed to flower, and then
wither and die, spreading seed
for next year's flowers—
temporary splendors.

The rains, flowers, and seasons—
our physical lives and our dreams—
come and go like waves.
Devotees are blessed to see
everything in perspective:
the knowledge of all truths
is the real spiritual manna
of service to Krishna
and his humble, wise devotees.
Our aim is always to remember
Krishna amidst beauty and sorrow,
to let everything teach us
about our supernatural, eternal home
of celebration—the blissful
land of love, of deathless rejoicing.
Obtaining this goal is
the real success of life.

Listening for Spring

Walking to my favorite secluded spot,
down the steep hill by the stream,
to listen—or try to listen—
to spring's whispered awakening:
the early bulbs blooming,
some trees budding,
creating a certain scent
in the air. It's a subtle feeling.

I take my seat,
retrieve my journal and pen,
and, as if on cue, the crows
also arrive, cawing noisily
up the ridge, flying from tree to tree.
It seems they have no purpose
except to distract and test me.
What can I do but smile?

Admittedly, their cawing isn't pleasing
to my ear and their forms
aren't esthetically uplifting.
My tendency is to be annoyed.
I have to let go of that,
though they are not my favorite.
I remember them in trash heaps.
They're the *Bhagavata's* example
of the lowly, the opposite of the swan.
Yet, every creature has its place
in Krishna's world—like it or not!

At this point in the poem,
they are gone. With the returning quiet
of the forest come more subtle sounds,
near and far: frogs splashing downstream
at the pond, dogs barking somewhere,
muffled in the distance,
a car roaring farther away.
The threatening dark clouds above
make good on their potential,
bringing slow raindrops.
The rush of the wind announces
it may be a downpour.
This time of year is unpredictable!

My umbrella goes up.
I'm hoping to wait out the storm.
Now, with only the rain's sound,
I try to keep dry, surrounded by wind
that chills my hands and face.
I smell wet leaves
and the stream's speed increases.
Oh, the simple pleasures in life.
In nature, without new styles,
we only have to show up
with our desire, attention,
and curious eyes.
So much can be learned—
never boring, always something
new to discover (without or within)!

As suddenly as it came,
the rain abates.
Now, there's only the sound
of drops from branches
and the soft, indirect light
coming through the clouds—
mystical, enchanting—
heightening the moss's green,
contrasting with the grey
and brown of bare trees,
drawing attention to the bark
so varied in texture.
Soon, spring's full force
will paint the forest
in that special, intense spring green—
Krishna says *I am spring*!

External, Internal Seasons

Winter overcomes our pleasant memories
with its chilling, damp, windy, grey mood.
Time stands still and the leafless trees cry.
Even though we know spring will come,
we still wonder how we'll survive.

Now that winter is fading,
the luscious bulbs burst forth.

I am reminded how my previous life
without a spiritual quest leading to Krishna
seemed purposeless, ominous, and dark.

I was given inexplicable (by material logic) knowing:
in my great need, I realized what was missing
from my life. The spiritual dimension
called to me, awakening hope and unheard-of enthusiasm,
giving me the willingness to travel uncharted roads.

I could feel my life's winter ending.
I knew a season of joy and blooms
was right before my eyes.
I only needed to find the right key
to unlock a spiritual door never dreamed of before.

Somehow, then, life told me, *yes!*,
whereas before it always said, *no!*
So, a normally dull, confused youth
became a spiritual seeker with purpose—
a surprise to my family and friends.

Previously, life was only boring,
simply something to be endured
or to be distracted from.
Now, life was a mystery at every step,
something to be solved and lived joyously.
I finally had a path for success.

II.
Yet, even on the path of joy—
of perpetual dance and song—
there are still seasons to embrace.
The ups and downs of spiritual practice
are where we find new layers of purification.

To the tired spiritual traveler,
the spiritual path is an oasis.
Finding it, we may think our work is done.
We can rest in peace and happiness
since we know the truth.

Although we have the key
to open the door, we still must enter.
Inside, we find another journey awaits:
the inner voyage of introspection,
letting go, prayer, and discipline.

Time tests us with all-around changes.
Externally and internally, adjustments are required.
We must let go of the superficial, what no longer works.
We must discover deeper foundations
and eliminate whatever's unessential and shallow.

Initially, the path to Krishna seems
black and white. It can be held in our hands,
and simply by repeating the magic formula,
we're amazed at the transformative power,
not anticipating its effects or our growth.

With more knowledge and realization,
openness and yearning reveal
a nuanced, deep spiritual path,
not always either-or, but sometimes both.
With increased capacity, the next mountain looms.

The Rama Green of Spring Inspires

Krishna is "flower bearing spring,"
an easy time for reflection.
I'm encouraged by saintly company—
both the season and association
are heart-opening. By accepting
the spiritual goal—not just officially,
but determinedly—the world changes it's perspective
toward us. Everyone becomes our teacher.
No situation is unfavorable.
Informed by scriptural study,
taught by spiritual adepts,
we stay fixed in practice,
regardless of our work.

With hands and knees on the moist Earth,
biological grounding's created.
Attuned to country living,
strengthened by Bhakti practice—

in the world, but not of it—
I'm present in my body,
focused on my heart and soul.
Innate talents are activated—
natural software and hardware—
fostering sensitivity and awareness,
insightful hearing, feeling, and sensing.
I'm appreciating divine potential
instead of remaining repressed,
out of touch with life lessons,
or merely sensually distracted.

Overcast skies augment colors,
increasing spring green's iridescence,
bringing my thoughts to Lord Rama
and inspiring me on his appearance day
to appreciate nature's beauty as he did.
Though he was banished to the forest,
Sita and Lakshmana, his loyal family,
together created a forest festival,
teaching us to seek the positive
and make the best of all difficulties.
Though discouraged, we should never give up.
We should seek the goal till we find it,
adopting the seeker's quest,
making it our highest ideal,
practicing Bhakti in love—
for Krishna, gurus, and *Vaishnava*s—
finding our way home.

On Meeting Life with a Smile and Spiritual Eyes, Wide Awake

Forces of material nature
are a two-edged sword,
dishing out physical miseries while
simultaneously remaining beautiful and sublime—
Krishna's purposeful energy.

Distant thunder approaches, darkening the sky.
Winds majestically allow the trees to dance.
While squirrels eat mulberries,
the crows chew wild, bitter cherries.
We sit, waiting for the main show.

Everything follows natural laws:
the *Gita* tells us matter combines into eight energies.
Krishna supplies rain, sun, earth, and sky.
Flowers bloom and trees tower over all.
Humans ponder why mosquitoes bite.

Life forms must obey their bodies.
Humans are on parole. We can decide
to remain physically bound—forced and restricted—
or to become spiritually joyful by agreeing to serve.
When we become a Bhakta, everything teaches us.

Huge raindrops commence the drama.
The loud roar of millions of droplets
fills the darkened sky, intensified by thunder

rumbling across the heavens, then exploding.
Such exciting storms are never the same!

Wind increases. Rain falls at warp speed.
The tempest is on top of us.
Lightening immediately follows thunder.
Material nature: dangerous, full of wonder—
will we be crushed or survive to tell?

Our body may or may not be protected.
The house could be blown away, or stay.
Yet, Krishna promises to protect the soul.
Once on Bhakti's path, we will remain.
Krishna carries our lack, preserves our love.

II.
We're a unit of serving tendency,
meant to give, sacrifice, and love,
given freedom to invest our heart
which carries us to the next body or
to the nectarous land of heart service.

Divorced, distressed souls, uplifted and saved
from a dangerous place, brought to Krishna's embrace.
Struggling for existence, free in the dance of *kirtan;*
lost in illusion, found in service.
Everything is favorable for divine upliftment.

The ocean in the drop—
eternity in the moment—
life's secret before our eyes:

one step begins a journey to Krishna.
A devotee's blessing opens our soul.

Complacency and lethargy: the enemies.
Caught up in day-to-day struggles,
we lose heart, thinking progress impossible —
but, *NO*! Regroup. Rekindle the spiritual fire.
Recall determination. Find good company.

If not now, when?
Tomorrow is always out of reach.
Today we must do better —
chanting, reading, praying more —
since we may die watching a movie!

Don't defeat yourself by failures.
Cast them aside, begin anew —
remember faith, spiritual feeling, taste.
Help is always available if we ask.
Be courageous; don't settle for mediocrity!

III.
What an opulence to sit on the porch
watching the storm build, then deliver.
Much of life is just showing up, awake:
observing, thinking, seeing, and feeling Krishna —
the perfect arranger — reminding us of himself.

The storm passes; normality returns:
forest serenity, soothing calm.
Tree frogs sing in joy.

Plants, flowers, and trees drink their fill.
What have I learned?

Life is truly a great wonder.
Years of spiritual practice bear fruit.
Imperfect? We are, but we have shelter:
enlivening literature, beautiful Deities,
 satisfying service, and a superlative goal!

The Joy of Rain

Have you ever been down,
then cheered up by the rain?
Listening to a soothing downpour,
watching the wonder of water
with mist caressing your face,
you feel Krishna amidst beauty.
Sharing your grief, the sky cries tears.
Thunder shakes the house.
Wow! God is great—
powerful, and yet, our dearest friend.

As if to dramatize
my sorrow with a solution,
the rain and wind increase,
moistening everything.

Grabbing my prasad,
I retreat inside, smiling.
Going to the sunroom—
today a "rainroom"—
I am very grateful
for so many blessings.

Most days in my life
are sunny and bright—
not Pollyanna,
but like shining steel tempered
by a painful upbringing and polished
by my awakening in Bhakti.
I struggled for material identity, then
found my service and love.
Though some days it rains on my parade,
light always emerges.

Taking shelter of Krishna
in good times and bliss
allows us to embrace sadness,
disappointment, reverses, and illness.
Whatever comes our way is mercy,
so we study the scriptures
and hear others' successful struggles.
We experience a varied life
of ups, downs, and in-betweens,
our joy always in Krishna.

I pray to remember Krishna
in all conditions, with all persons.

With our beautiful and kind Deities,
the blessing of our daily *japa* and *kirtan*,
incredibly insightful and wise scriptures,
and inspiring saintly association—
practicing gratitude,
counting our blessings,
it is difficult to remain down for long.
I simply remember my soul and Krishna.

Thank you Lord
for opportunities to serve,
to love, to give, to aspire for Bhakti,
to appreciate the saintly,
to believe in my potential
as a soul in human dress,
to learn humility and spiritual confidence
and the joy of a spiritual goal.

Listen to the Earth: Be a Giver

A week of rain
with more on the way,
a full morning
of *sadhana* and prayer—
my country spot calls me.
It's favorable for contemplation and writing,

a secluded place by the creek
that inspires many themes to share.

As we prepare for prayer
by remembering our dependence
on our gurus and Krishna,
I prepare for the wetness.
Donning rain gear and an umbrella—
a practical, yet symbolic staff—
I'm reminded of the *Vedic* knowledge
that supports and directs me.

A special quality
of nature's green
on overcast days—
defused light looks otherworldly.
That iridescent, exciting green
seems to vibrate vitality.
My redwood forest days
first revealed this wonder.

After so much rain,
the trees and ground are soaked.
The smell of wet leaves and
mushrooms are everywhere.
Though the rain has stopped,
a secondhand rain continues—
water drip, drip, dripping
from leaf to leaf, to the earth.

Such soothing sounds
meet the flowing noise of the creek,
now muddy brown.
It's flowing fast now with new life.
Sitting amidst the trees, I feel them
all vibrating growth and life.
Is that *Om* I hear them chanting?
They sing their song of peace.

It's an amazing experience to be open,
to just close my eyes to receive, to listen
to the water sounds
sending out love and blessings.
Everyone and everything's a teacher.
I receive so much from Krishna's nature,
meditating on the supportive Earth,
a supreme giver of necessities.

A *Vedic* verse teaches:
All wealth comes from the Earth.
So, we're glad to receive her bounty,
but slow to reciprocate and honor her.
The Earth, like a cow,
teaches us that, to be full,
we give in love to others.
Miserliness is hording.

For all of us, this is the question:
how do I increase my giving
as a way to spiritual attainment
based on soul-love awakening?

The answer: follow the greatest model
of Krishna with his devotees,
joyfully sustaining and inspiring all
by giving heart and soul.

Nothing extraordinary here,
just sharing basic "Life 101"—
simple, yet profound truths.
If we take the time to listen
amidst our busy, chaotic lives—
to sit in nature and reflect, chant,
and read the *Gita* and *Bhagavatam*—
we can remember life's purpose.

Appreciating the Blessings of Nature

This is my first blog poem, written on September 11, 2007:

We "own" four acres of land (the bank thinks they own it, but it really belongs to Krishna) in the foothills of North Carolina. It is near to Hanging Rock State Park, one hour north of Winston-Salem.

This country area is quite beautiful, the peaceful environment conducive for spiritual practice. After living in the suburbs of Baltimore for fourteen years, having all spiritually-minded devotee neighbors is an unbelievable opulence.

Sometimes I go down to the bottom of our land and chant,

read, or just commune with nature. Here is a poem I wrote during one such occasion:

Idyllic meditation spot
at the bottom of our land—
I sit by the creek hearing
sounds of winds and birds.

The deep and light
green of the forest,
the rich smell of earth
after days of rain—

coming here nourishes
an unused part of me:
my intuitive nature and
need to commune with the earth.

Even though this land
was cleared many years ago,
many large trees remain,
giving great joy to my psyche.

These large, old-growth trees
are "real trees" to me,
priceless beings
living hundreds of years.

I come here occasionally
if I have chanting to do

on my *japa* beads at midday
and I have the extra time.

I daydream of making
a secret discovery of treasure,
finding a clue to *Vedic* culture,
or talking to nature spirits.

I am always at the center
of my wandering mind,
very far from being absorbed
in Krishna's pastimes.

I, me, and mine
are still often my focus—
the enjoying propensity.
I offer my mind to Krishna secondarily.

Something is better than nothing,
yet the goal of chanting
is to love Krishna, free from false ego,
and identify his purpose as my own.

At present I can only read about
or pray to obtain my high ideal,
while I honestly feel it will take lifetimes
to revive my eternal serving nature.

As I think and write,
flies buzz around my head,

and the light frequently changes
as the sun goes behind clouds.

I am grateful that Krishna has
provided me such a beautiful place
to chant, write, pray, and think—
how merciful that blue boy is to me!

To contrast my first blog poem above, here is one I recently wrote in the fall of 2015.

Receiving Nature's Aesthetic Wisdom

Salt-scented wind forever blows.
The all-powerful sun runs the show.
Unimaginable tons of water float
as easily as we breathe and sigh.
Clouds artistically decorate the vast sky—
billowy, multi-colored cotton balls
shapeshifting with the mind's desires.
They amaze and delight my imagination,
fostering creativity and contemplation.
Oh, the wonder of being alive and aware,
of having the time to be and simply stare

without distractions or appointments.
Only constant nature forces
an ubiquitous *Aha!* So profound, yet
often missed in our busyness.
Here or there—we're always going somewhere,
but we're not arriving at our true longing.

A tiny description of the immeasurable Universal (worldly) Form of God according to the essence of all Vedic literature, the Shrimad Bhagavatam:

O King, the rivers are the veins of the gigantic body, the trees are the hairs of his body, and the omnipotent air is his breath. The passing ages are his movements, and his activities are the reactions of the three modes (or qualities) of material nature.

... the clouds which carry water are the hairs on his head, the terminations of days or nights are his dress, and the supreme cause of material creation is his intelligence. His mind is the moon, the reservoir of all changes.

The principle of matter (mahat-tattva) is the consciousness of the omnipresent Lord, as asserted by the experts, and Rudradeva (Shiva) is his ego. The horse, mule, camel, and elephant are his nails, and wild animals and all quadrupeds are situated in the belt zone of the Lord. Varieties of birds are indications of his masterful artistic sense.

Manu, the father of mankind, is the emblem of his standard intelligence, and humanity is his residence. The celestial species of human beings, like the Gandharvas, Vidyadharas, Caranas, and angels, all represent his musical rhythm, and the demoniac soldiers are representations of his wonderful prowess.
Shrimad Bhagavatam, 2.1.33–26

The sun illuminates both internally and externally by expanding its radiation; similarly, the Supreme Personality of Godhead, by expanding his universal form, maintains everything in the creation both internally and externally.
Shrimad Bhagavatam, 2.6.17

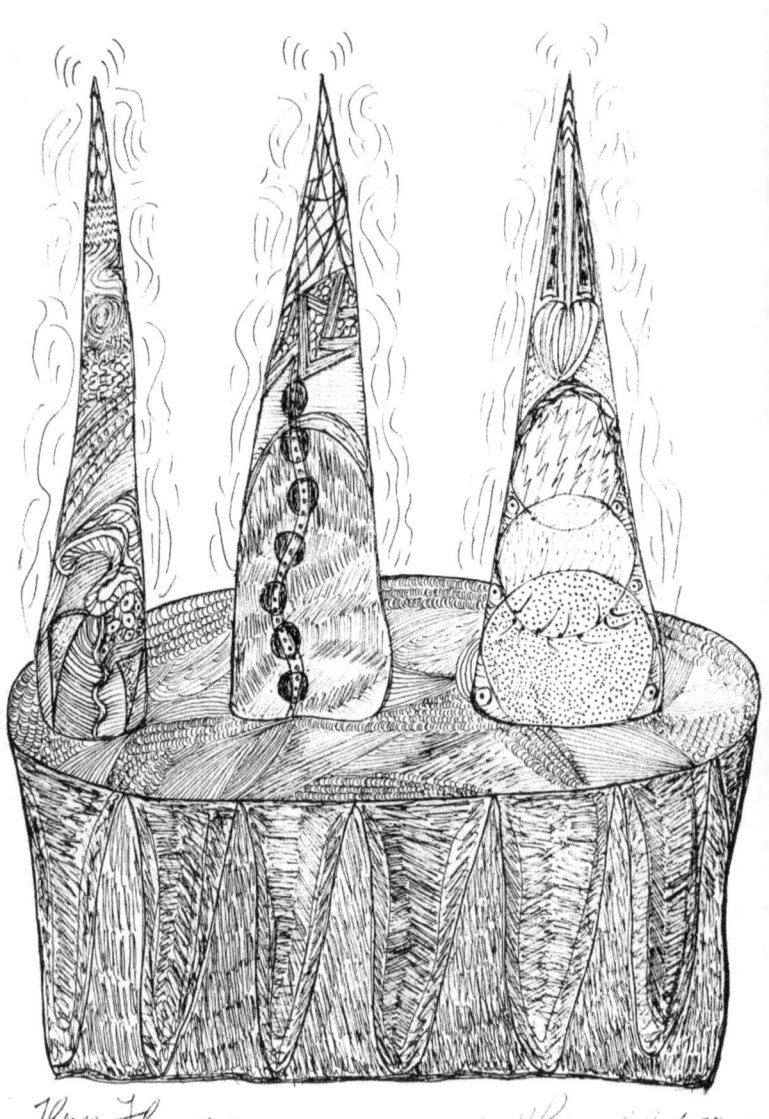

Three Flames

Chapter 3

RELATIONSHIPS

Love is as love does.
Love is a verb, not a noun.

Everything that irritates about others can
lead us to an understanding of ourselves.
Carl Jung

Everyone thinks of others
according to their own position.
Shrila Prabhupada

Fool for Love

Is it really so surprising
that anyone—even a mentor—
could be a fool
for love and intimacy?

So many are affected
by the lure of infatuated love,
the need to be understood, appreciated,
and accepted by a dear friend.

Whenever I hear
or make a criticism,
I know what I see
is within me, at least potentially.

Criticizing another is
putting myself above them,
forgetting my own defects,
blind spots, and vulnerabilities.

Sometimes the loudest judgments
arise from the hidden secrets
of those with similar problems,
those who fear that very part in themselves.

Certainly there are standards
to be encouraged and upheld,
yet the deficiencies we notice in others
often say more about us than them.

Is our first reaction
anger and indignation,
or do we feel compassion
and think to reach out to help?

We are so quick
to forget the value of a person,
the good they have done,
speaking their infamy with four mouths.

As Relationships Change, So Must We

Relationships change in time—
relationships with others and with ourselves—
though universal energy sustains all.
It's the background and resting place.
Our most basic relationship
in physical life is with our body and mind.

We have been sentenced
for a number of years
in the prison house of matter,
dressed in physical and mental garments,
a stock of karma—good and bad—
making us feel happy or sad.

While living in the world,
we discover matter's limitations.
Scripture and experience help,
along with spiritual practice.
We're required to make mental adjustments
as cherished attachments are shattered.

Without spiritual understanding,
the gradual decline and demise
of the structure of happiness
we have labored hard
to erect and maintain
brings frustration and regret.

Like most people,
I took for granted
"normal" bodily functions.
Now they're declining and screaming
for attention, teaching me
I'm not the master.
I'm a servant of material conditions.

I have always loved to walk
and commune with nature.
I thought this was my right,
but now my knee pain teaches me
that walking is really a gift,
a blessing for which to be grateful!

In our life, we can be unconscious.
We can act ignorantly, habitually,

thinking we are the center—*but no!*
But alas, blinded, we can't see evidence
of immortality—*but wait!* We *can* see,
through a spiritual lens, the eternal soul!

Observing nature and life
instructs the thoughtful seeker:
plants and animals are forced
to suffer in self-ignorance,
while humans are blessed with life
that can be used for spiritual freedom.

A combative, controlling, exploitive attitude
won't reveal life's secrets. Nature will seem silent,
mechanical, and lifeless. It will seem almost
within the grasp of our understanding, yet
it will confound us
with new mysteries and shattered theories.

The universe has its own
purpose beyond
our tiny selfish interest.
The Infinite becomes knowable
to the finite who approach
in the spirit of giving and serving.

Understanding the Infinite's purpose for us and knowing
there's infinite purpose beyond us—the Creative God,
our Source—we bow down in supplication,
praying to align ourselves with his will.

We're uplifted in lasting happiness,
so elusive before, once only temporarily visited.

Sitting on a huge boulder,
writing by waterfalls for hours,
I make a metaphor for rear-end pain. But also,
as others walk, I contemplate my life,
seeing it in the laws of nature
amidst the forest's beauty.

Creation's charm and splendor
point the godly seeker
toward the Source,
as much as the beauty of
a painting makes us curious
to know the painter.

As I write, I'm reminded by my poem
that spiritual practice isn't an idle hobby.
It needs to show up
in all situations and teach us
to find the treasure in each moment's lesson.
It needs to awaken us to what is!

Dreaming a Quest up the Relationship Mountain

Amidst thoughts about my past, about how my past relates to my present, I've thought and felt deeply about relationships — relationships I've had and relationships for which I've endeavored. In response to my contemplation, I wrote this poem. It's full of angst and intense emotion about my failed relationships. It's full of disappointment about my successful relationships, and it's also full of my hopes and aspirations.

While most of us value relationships highly, often they are the source of our greatest distress and sadness. Everyone wants to be loved and understood, but we are never loved and understood quite to the degree we want. Even in what seem to be the best relationships, we may be separated from our beloved by death, debilitating disease, divorce, mental imbalance, or dementia.

Examining the depth of my capacity to love, I ask: *Who in this world can I love and understand fully? Who is capable of fully accepting my heart's gifts?* At least in my experience, no one can completely satisfy the desire to love or to be loved in return.

This could be depressing, or it could be a turning point that orients us in the direction of a spiritual goal. In my case, my goal is to love and serve God — whom I call *Radha-Krishna* — with my spiritual heart and soul. My negative impetus for spiritual love and service is bitter experience — disappointment — in worldly relationships. My positive impetus: taste in spiritual practices, and eventually, pure love for Krishna, *prema*.

All relationships and dealings with people and things of this world are meant to point us in the direction of God, the source of everything, the complete object of our love. Our desire for unending, ever-increasing love can only be fulfilled by the One who can accept our love unlimitedly. For me, that One is Krishna, who's said to be the fountainhead of all relationships (*rasas*) and the cynosure of the eye, heart, and soul.

I.
I'm a disabled person climbing
a mountain: my words are my hammer,
my feelings are my spikes and rope.
I don't know if they'll hold or help me up,
give me a grip for a steady journey, help me
avoid the trolls who would like to hurl me down.
I only have my effort and a prayer—an aspiration
to reach the top—where I'll find
the entrance to your Self-universe.

I'm at your threshold, a decorated, scented, strong door—
your appearance and persona—at once inviting and bewildering. And still, entering that door is another beginning. Now, I must pass guards, moats, and walls.
Finally approaching your interior castle, I have no certainty
of success, but I have the hope of finding
your heart's inner chambers.

II.
Our hearts are unpredictable oceans.
Even *we* don't fully understand them, but we try
to make sense of one another honestly.
We find many possibilities
to explain the heart's language—
associations from the past,

words of the mind's logic.
It isn't an easy task to decipher the code,
and it requires generosity and kindness,
openness and strong willingness
to believe in what's possible,
to believe that blessings come
unexpectedly and push us to grow,
to embrace our differences—we never know!

III.
Relationships are like mirrors
where we project our ideals or notice
our own faults in another.
Infatuation and projection confound
our longing for love. As if by magic, our hearts
seem to awaken with feelings
for another whom we hardly know.
From where is this coming? And how? We can't fathom
the answer. There is a hidden spiritual reason:
this world is a reflection of the spiritual plane.
So, simply because we give ourselves permission,
a spark of our original nature manifests
as the oneness love generates.
Our soul is a unit of love, desiring to express itself
in service, desiring to give itself to God and every living being.
But, right now, it's covered by the body and mind, so
the ego decides who will be loved, and who will not.

IV.
Is our relationship like a game of chess?
If I lose, am I dismissed

by rules and feelings I don't know?
Please help me out here.
Give me a chance
to obtain some leniency passes, some
"Get Out of Checkmate Free" tickets and
"Get Out of Relationship Jail Free" cards.
Or perhaps, you could gift me a rewind button,
like the one in the movie *Groundhog Day*.
Then, I could try again to make sense
of my ramblings and feelings
and find benefit in it all for us both.
We both require mental reassurance to protect
our self-interest because unconditional love is a myth
(at least in material consciousness).

V.
Silence can speak volumes
as a response. It creates infinite space
between and around us.
We decide how to fill the void arbitrarily
because it can mean anything.
It leaves me to ponder the code:
Is it a gift to contemplate? Or is it
a punishment for worthlessness?
It's gloomy in the prison of my mind,
where positive and negative judgments
are contrary convictions, simultaneous life-sentences.

VI.
If you and I are separate countries,
and your heart is the capital,

can I apply for a visa to your capital
where I hope to create a permanent embassy?
You don't know whether to trust me or to assume
that I'm mad on an inexplicable quest, but
can we find common ground?
Can we find mutual faith, hope, and desire,
knowing the unexpected
can be the hand of destiny?
Some people come into our lives to teach
(or we to teach them)
for a moment, month, or lifetime.

VII.
What we keep in our heart
(and thus who we give to)
is our greatest treasure.
Those who reside inside—
due to love or hate—
we are bound to meet again,
to work out our feelings
and pay back our karmic debts.
Yet, those with realized wisdom
love God primarily, prominently.
They travel to him by love's power,
loving others as part of the Supreme,
not trying to own or control them
because things and people come and go.

VIII.
As souls, we are a particle of Love, covered over
right now by biology's necessities. So, we want love,

directly or subconsciously, and we search for it
and compensate for its absence.
All we desire, all we give, all we receive—
the ground that paves our path—
is really disguised love, an indirect request for affection.
But, along the way to living in complete divine love
and service, we will gradually awaken to
the Supreme Love of our heart—one step, one mantra,
one prayer at a time.

> *Love feels no burden, thinks nothing of trouble, attempts what is above its strength, pleads no excuse of impossibility; for it thinks all things lawful for itself, and all things possible.*
> Thomas á Kempis

> *When love of Godhead is attained, love for all other beings automatically follows because the Lord is the sum total of all living beings.*
> From Shrila Prabhupada's introduction to
> *Shrimad Bhagavatam*

> *The basic principle of the living condition is that we have a general propensity to love someone. No one can live without loving someone else. This propensity is present in every living being. . . . The missing point, however, is where to repose our love so that everyone can become happy. . . . That missing point is* Krishna.
> From Shrila Prabhupada's preface to *The Nectar of Devotion*

Relationships Are Everything

Some complain
of difficulty getting along with others
who cause them pain, distress, and heartache.
Ah, they say, if they could get away
from others and be alone, just relax,
then they could experience some peace
and quiet. But if we really study
the universe, we find whatever exists,
conscious or inert, must be
in relationship to something else.

Everything has component parts—
from solar systems and planets
to the elements composing them:
earth, water, fire, air, and space;
living things and celestial bodies;
cells, DNA, atoms, and molecules;
mountains, streams, valleys,
plains, deserts, and oceans—
all have meaning by comparison
and relationship. Nothing stands alone,
though all is one in Krishna.
He manifests form and variety,
and we cannot *not* be
in correspondence to him, nor can even a speck
of existence exist outside his being.

To master one's self or life,
one must master relationships,

life's building blocks,
the keys to happiness and fulfillment,
mirrors to help us look at ourselves.

We are interdependent.
Independence is an illusion
from any angle of vision,
atomic or universal.
The ultimate truth:
we are part of God
who is the Center of our center,
the Life of our life,
Soul of our soul,
the glue that binds things
in relation to "other" things—
parts to parts, people to people.

True, lasting happiness
is found in playing the part
we were designed to play—
lovingly serving our Source,
and more intimately,
the Lord of our hearts.

The principle *Gaudiya Vaishnava* forms
of God, Radha & Krishna and
Gaura & Nitai, are never alone.
They're always surrounded
by loving servants—
friends, parents, or lovers.

Every type of relationship
finds rest in them.

For now, we have to rehearse
relating to others—people and devotees—
our spouse, child, friend, boss, guru,
teacher, student, or antagonist.
All relationships are practice.
We practice being loving, kind,
and compassionate. We practice choosing
to find the good, instead of focusing on
the blemishes. We practice seeing
who others—and we—really are.

We can't escape others
by false renunciation.
We must learn to get along
with all types of "others"—
even the lowest, meanest, and most selfish—
even those most conditioned to
this material world. To the great souls,
all can be teachers. All have the potential
to help uncover our sleeping soul,
to show us that from which we need
to be purified. We learn that
without relationships, we can't exist,
in this world or the next.

Failure Is the Pillar of Success—After Slipping, Again, Rise Up!

As I was about to embrace illusion,
yet again, the kind Lord revealed a vision:

On the road to me (Krishna)
failure is the pillar of success.
Why? Because you are on the path!
You have once seen
the error and terror of your worldly ways,
calling out to me for help
while drowning in miseries.

I heard you (remember?),
and gladly threw you a rope.
Your acceptance of it greatly pleased me!
Once you begin this spiritual quest
and grab that rope of grace,
it is forever yours.

No matter what reason caused you to start out,
you can't get off the path
back to me, which is your only hope.
This path is permanently
part of you; you will never be the same.
Know this as my mercy!

Before, you thought you were fine!
Now again, you're back on your feet
with new opportunities. Nonsense!

That's a lie! You are meant to be with me!
Don't you remember,
I am the love of your life,
the Soul of your soul?

You thought you could return
to your old life of enjoyment?
Ha! You think I would let you?
You think I would allow you to forget me
yet again in your sensual stupidity
after countless lifetimes of ignorance?
You think I would allow you to forget
you are mine and I am yours eternally?

After tasting the holy name's nectar
through service to my devotees,
nothing can ever compare
to the spiritual happiness you've savored.
Imperfect as you are, I have accepted you,
and my will never goes in vain.

You knew me as the goal!
But you stubbornly tried to forget.
Haven't you learned yet—
the senses are paths to death!
Really! Haven't you had enough?
Do you have to try yet again
the road of temptation?
Instead, take the road of redemption!

Can I tell you honestly?
If I do, will you accept me fully
as your friend and well-wisher?
I love you, now and always!
So forget the past!
I don't care about it.
Now only look toward your ideal:
union with me in eternal love.

Remember I am with you
birth after birth.
Though you have ignored me,
I will never give up on you,
even as you try in vain to enjoy
gross matter by repeatedly chewing
already chewed stalks of sugarcane.

I try to guide you.
If only you would listen,
turning just once toward me.
How long can we continue
down the path of the senses, the path
of countless varieties of species
with only slight differences? It's hope
against hope. You obstinately forget
that what you seek through your senses is me!

Pick yourself up, sleeping soul!
Rise up to my light!
I am here to help you!
I have sent my devotee to you

to train you to take my shelter,
to keep you on the path
where you'll finally gain the strength
and determination to come to me.

Don't ever be discouraged,
though you stumble and fall.
As long as you keep trying,
struggling to get up,
you will eventually remain
standing up strong, yet humble.
Don't accept defeat!
Don't give up, no matter what!

This time, your efforts
will be crowned with success.
Keep chanting and praying.
Study the scriptures.
Keep company with saints.
This time you will make it.

I have faith in you—
my devotee, have faith in *me*!

The Interior Castle; Saved from Quicksand

The Interior Castle
We want the same things:
to be loved, understood, valued.
It's only a question of degree—
Are we spiritually and psychologically healthy,
satisfied in spiritual practice and
satisfied with who we are? Or are we needy,
reeling from a dysfunctional past, meeting intense cravings
unhealthily, unable to uncover the soul's joy in service?

Desiring to share our inner life,
to be accepted for both our ideal and our darkness,
we're prevented access by mutual walls and ramparts—
false personalities that separate our castles.
We try to protect all from pain and hurt,
giving only limited access,
holding court with a scripted façade,
allowing none to enter our inner chambers.

We want to convey our feelings,
but few have the desire to hear.
Yet, we religiously pursue relationships
or retreat into inaccessible, locked towers.
We're punished for honesty, labeled as crazy.
Everyone has secret rules for love:
who gets to enter beyond which wall and how far,
who's cast into the moat, who's banished forever.

Saved from Quicksand
By taking inventory of our conditioned identity,
seeing our dark and shadowy constructs
as well as our highest material potential—
what pulls us down, what lifts us up—
with the help of spiritual practice, we can see clearly:
our desires only reflect our soul nature
yet fail to satisfy the mind and heart
until they're used to uncover our love for God.

Material distress and dissatisfaction have meaning,
pointing us in the transcendental direction
or pulling us down into further ignorance.
Spiritual wisdom reveals true solutions,
laying bare worldly infatuation and illusion—
the plane of temporal delusion where we repeatedly
try to find pleasure in stroking our spacesuit
rather than living uncovered as an eternal soul.

We must be convinced of our life's work and solution—
chanting the holy name, engaging in divine service,
hearing Bhakti scriptures—the ways of illumined life.
And from saintly company, we'll receive wise advice.
We must learn to look for Krishna's hand, his direction,
to do the needful *now*, keeping the goal in mind.
For desires and attachments, the way out is through.
From struggling against our conditions, we'll come to
joy, seeing the world as favorable for Bhakti.

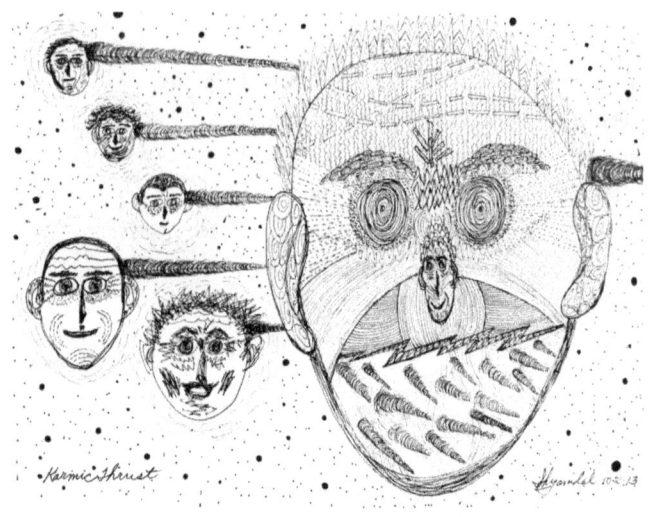

The Holy Grail of Relationships

Our soul identifies with a body—
physical needs, expansive desires,
loneliness, lacking—unhappy, we seek completion
through relationships.

Through princes and princesses, Disney shows us
the oneness of loving forgetfulness, the way of
covering our foolishly perceived deficiencies,
identifying our Self through projection.

We idolize, worship the "other"—
our covered, hidden self.

We think, *Now my life's beginning,*
whereas before I lived in the desert.
Finally, I'm rid of my sad story.
I've created a life worth living.
It seems it can't get any better.
I am living my dream!

Then suddenly, unexpectedly, we're forced out
of our ethereal mind-airplane,
and we're falling with no parachute.
Our crash scatters pieces of a life.

Our beautiful bubble bursts:
How could I have been so blind?
Alas, the secret's still withheld:
it was always about *me*.

My "love" was never about *giving* to my lover.
No, it was about unspoken rules and conditions,
unexpressed fine print, expectations and dramas, our past
damaged selves—all perceived through a skewed lens.

Childhood dramas, disappointments, past lives—
we endeavor to overcompensate.
Our parents are disguised as our spouse—
past issues, addressed now.

Our own deficiencies need to be resolved,
yet we stubbornly miss the point,
looking again for perfect love and support,
for the Holy Grail of drugs: romance.

We travel flower to flower
on the never-ending karmic quest,
or we give up in aggravation:
It's all sour grapes! All illusion and vanity.

Thinking, *Why me*,
we die dismayed, lamenting,
frustrated that our soul mate
became Dracula and ate our heart.

If only we can discover
lovely, enchanting Krishna,
whose endearing love is the active rest
for all souls. In him, our relationships are purified.

In him, all situations are favorable;
our life and our desires are transformed.
Focusing on the Supreme Shelter,
we find complete engagement for our heart.

Appealing, unending love
centered on the hearts of Radha and Krishna—
Krishna's flute sound sustains us
in the dance of perfection.

Embraced by our true love,
ever-increasingly fulfilled,
we know happiness beyond compare—
never a dull moment in eternity.

Relationships, Togetherness

Relationships, togetherness,
connection, and sharing
are not merely the spices of life.
They're the foundations of animation,
the juice and energy that sustain us
beyond merely existing and maintaining.
The celebration of we—us, our, the many—
points us in the direction of selfless service.

Human beings especially crave another
to share life and make it easier
through joys and sorrows,
familial trials and achievements—
another to understand our inner self
(as far as even *we* can),
another to believe in us and really care despite
our imperfections, another to accept
our love and affection.

The double-edged relationship sword
lifts us up in hope and joyous support
or stabs us in our most vulnerable part.
Though wounded yet again,
we find solitude too austere a punishment.
So, at a risk, we set sail again
to the land of heart connection
with eternal hope for success.

As hard as we endeavor,
true friends are rare.
Yet, the failures are worth the gifts
of trying and learning more.
Many people have unspoken rules.
If we break them, we are dismissed.
There's no opportunity to explain our self,
no second chance.

Thrashed on the rocks of rejection,
we have to lick our wounds,
wondering what happened
and how to remove the dagger
thrust deeply in our bosom.
Yet, their door is locked shut,
and we have to move on, accepting
cruel fate in the form of counterfeit friends.

Even while we understand:
disappointment and pain confirm
transcendence, Godly service,
is really the key to our lasting happiness,
to the fulfillment of our soul—
still, we require soothing support
from like-minded souls.

The mystery of relationships
hints at ultimate reality
and acts as a mirror to show us our selves.
If we are not blinded by affection

or repulsed by hurt or anger,
those close to us teach us well,
not only about our light,
but also about our darkness.

There is no static oneness
since the spirit of God is everywhere.
Nothing exists without something else —
even an island is in the ocean.
The universe, variegation within oneness,
points to the spiritual source:
all souls in relationship to one another,
in loving service to Krishna.

Painful Impetus for Spiritual Practice: Good Grief!

Restrictions, limitations, impositions —
though my heart doesn't like them,
they're the rules of the body and mind
experienced by suffering, embodied souls.
A difficult past and present issues —
my own and others' combined —
bring me pain and regret that others
can't deal with me.

I'm forced to walk a tightrope
since conditioning rules my identity.

This is true even for devotees in Bhakti
who endeavor to awaken spiritually.
So, in spite of relationship upheavals,
I have to adapt and pray,
seeing all interpersonal difficulties
as impetus for spiritual practice.

Relationships disclose our issues.
We act, and others react.
It's like they're holding up a mirror,
revealing areas in which we need work,
illuminating our blind spots
along with our unhealed heart.
So we need others to help us
disconnect from our sad story.

I want to love and be loved,
but if a negative reaction comes,
regardless of the apparent cause,
I have to take full responsibility
rather than blaming others.
No one lives in a vacuum.
Relationships are about two.
I can only change myself.

Withdrawing the hooks of my energy,
not demanding reciprocation for my love,
aspiring to give love spiritually and prayerfully
with no expectations or conditions,
now I can unplug from selfish attachments,
do my best to love Krishna first,

and come to the spiritual platform,
seeing all souls with equanimity.

The Power of Grace in Meeting Our Guru

When the student is ready,
the guru is sent to help.
By the grace of Shri Krishna,
our spiritual life is revived.

Compelled by karma, wandering
throughout the vast universe,
sometimes we're a great demigod,
sometimes a lowly bug.

Out of thousands and millions
of lost souls traversing bodies,
one is especially blessed
to receive the seed of Bhakti.

Then, life after life,
spiritual progress is made
until one loves Krishna completely
and has no need for this world.

Everything begins by a saint's blessing,
sometimes unknowingly given.

Then, good, saintly company
changes one's nature and interests.

We're like a cold iron rod
placed in our guru's roaring fire.
Gradually we heat to red-hot and become
non-different from the fire.

The fire continues to blaze,
consuming all fuel
until all karma is finished.
Then, one offers one's Self entirely.

How long the process takes
depends on the urgency of our necessity.
Is one detoured by offenses,
becoming cold, or does one make the fire blaze?

The fire is kept alive
by pure hearing of scripture
and chanting of the holy name,
by humbly serving Guru and Krishna.

Both grace and effort are required.
We endeavor our best,
yet we humbly acknowledge
mercy is always in the background.

Our spiritual life begins by grace. Then,
it's sustained by a blessing—spiritual practice—and

determination—an effect of grace—that keeps us on course. Finally, by grace, we return to Krishna.

When we see men [or women] of a
contrary character,
we should turn inwards
and examine ourselves.
Confucius

The best mirror
is an old friend.
George Herbert

I bid him look into
the lives of men
as though into a mirror,
and from others to take
an example for himself.
Terence

Honest criticism is hard to take,
particularly from a relative,
a friend, an acquaintance,
or a stranger.
Franklin P. Jones

First keep the peace
within yourself,
then you can also
bring peace to others.
Thomas á Kempis

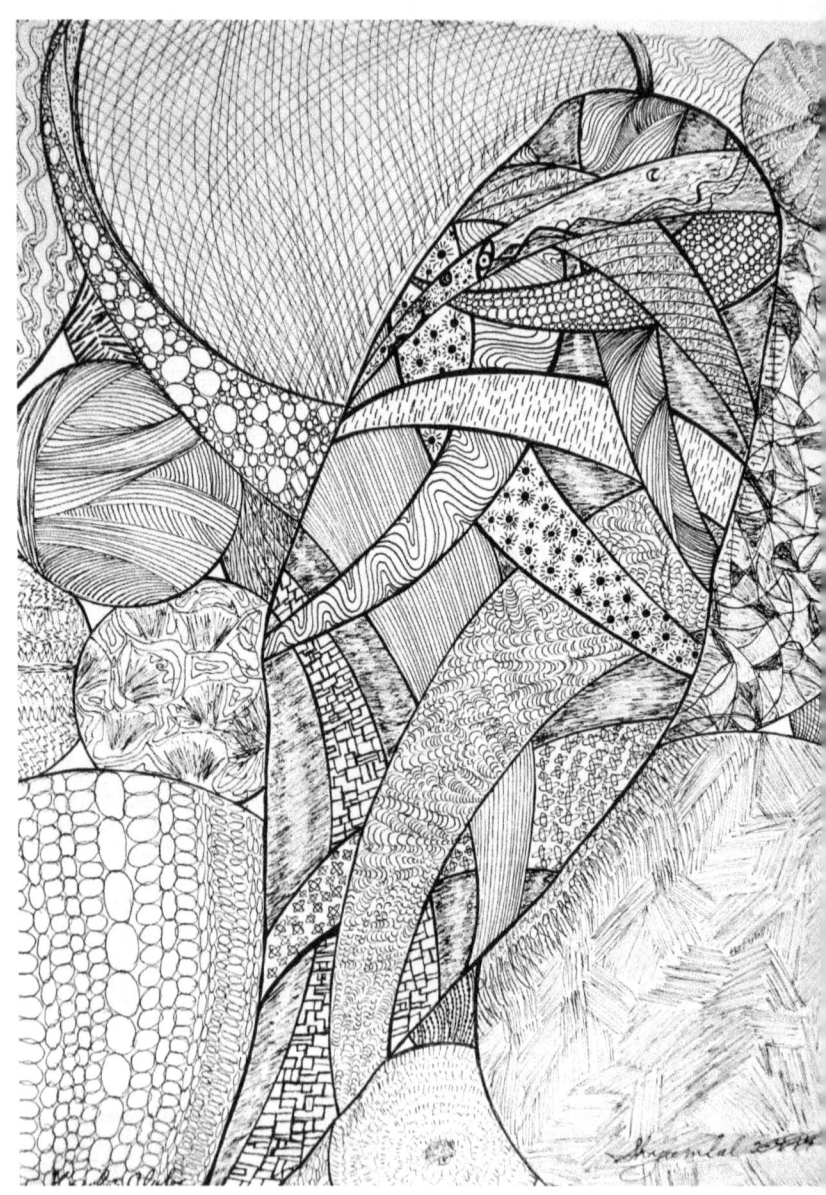

Chapter 4

SPIRITUAL PERSPECTIVES

A true yogi observes me in all beings and also sees every being in me. Indeed, the self-realized person sees me, the same Supreme Lord, everywhere. / For one who sees me everywhere and sees everything in me, I am never lost, nor is he ever lost to me.
Bhagavad Gita, 6.29–30

Classroom of Life 101

Many purposes are served
when our life events instruct.
Karma plays out,
yet Krishna teaches us.
Life, the master teacher—
learn to read its signs.
Attitudes determine labels:
good, bad, or sublime.
Any lessons learned today?
Here are some of mine:

I.
The ground browns, cracks.
Leaves turn yellow, drop.
Summer heat bakes—
sweltering, withering 'shine—
unusually hot and dry.
Every creature hopes for water.
Trees open their arms.
Roots grow deeper, searching.
Dew helps the grass, a taste.
Heads all look upward, expectant,
but some plants die, distraught.
Yet, they still give seeds for next year.
Can you hear the thirsty conversation?
Air breathes disappointment,
while the wise know rain will come.
Experience teaches confidence—
time brings thundershowers, life.

One can only wait.
Patience and hope are virtues.
Only humans can pray
in gratitude, building faith
that Krishna maintains.

II.
Imagine you felt Bhakti
(love and service for Krishna)
was your water and air—
that which sustains you.
How much effort and time
would you give for spiritual endeavor?
Oh, such intense eagerness
is the price for *prema* (Krishna's love).
We must always see service opportunities
instead of opportunities for sensual fulfillment,
since matter promises greatly
but serves only appetizers,
never the soul's full meal.
Understand your soul and God.
Change your aim and vision.
Know your true nourishment to be
Krishna, your dearest well-wisher and friend.

III.
Bhakti is water for the soul.
It gives true fulfillment,
happiness beyond the senses,
the feeling of going home.
Accepting Krishna's name

restores our true nature
and gives faith, love, and service.
You must decide your direction;
no one can do it for you.
Choose your path carefully,
seeing life as a spiritual journey,
gaining steadiness through wisdom
since reason can't touch the heart.
Only spiritual experience lasts.
Collect drops of nectar
from the ocean of devotion,
taking pleasure in service,
fixed on Krishna's love.

Is Life, or Am I, Complex or Simple?

So many opinions; so little time:
Are we, or is life
very complex
or very simple?

Both! Depending
on our nature and perspective.

A person or their life is simple or complex
according to their conditioned nature,

which could be a blessing or curse
in different circumstances.

Simple people think complex people
speak way too many words,
using too many colors or possessions
to hide life with endless distractions.

Complicated, complex-thinking people
will never accept simple explanations,
thinking them incomplete or
just too, well, simple to be adequate.

Matter seems more tangible to some
who think experimentation and conjecture
will unlock the secrets to controlling nature,
revealing our heart's desires.

Yet, for the trained eye, spirit
is primal, essential, foundational—
at once basic and simple, yet hidden.
Exploitation covers spiritual understanding.

Materially complicated people
make everything complex.
Simple or uncluttered spiritual people
find the essence and underlying purpose.

My guru, Prabhupada, taught
Krishna consciousness is simple

for the simple, but complicated
for the crooked or materialistic.

Spiritual texts can satisfy our intellect
or distract. The point is to soften the heart
by awakening the soul's Krishna *prema*. Then,
we'll manifest kindness and compassion for all.

Spiritual life is logical,
though ultimately trans-rational.
Complexity and simplicity are only useful
when they allow the soul to come out.

Begin where you are—don't fret!
Surrender complexity or simplicity
to gain understanding
of your identity in connection with Krishna.

How can the finite
know the infinite?
Only by infinite's grace, which humbles
both what's simple and complex.

Beyond the Land of Death and Doubt—
The Homeland of the Heart, Vrindavan

I.
The Iron Age of Quarrel (*Kali*),
the machine or garbage age,
glorifies technology
along with those who can run it,
proclaiming them most interesting,
important, and even supreme
among things and persons.

In our jaded view
of the "olden days" before technology,
we consider the no-tech times backwards,
primitive, and uncivilized
since today we are
much better off—
smarter, more sophisticated.

We don't consider that
when the power is off,
we have no clue
what to do or how to live.
In some cases,
humans without advanced technology
become worse than wild beasts.

Most modern problems
come from misuse of technology,
from trying to "improve"

or overcome the natural order,
creating so-called shortcuts.
In the name of "easy living,"
we create a complicated life.

We're dependent on artificial,
scarce resources, creating war and strife,
valuing man-made systems without gratitude to
God. Man's ego wants to think he is
making life better. His false pride inflated
by arrogance and violence, he thinks he can outsmart
natural laws while bragging about it.

II.
There is something within our soul
that is never satisfied
by the material status quo.
A fire burns inside,
inspiring us to reject
the laws of limitation, igniting
our desire for unconditional freedom.

Our veiled spiritual hankering fuels us
to push the envelope. We want
to have no restrictions,
to write our own rules.
We imagine transcending gravity,
soaring like a bird, diving
into the ocean, and entering the Earth.

Traveling through space at light's speed,
we revel in our brain's capacity
to understand, though we don't understand
life's purpose. We aspire to conquer
the elements, to go beyond
disease, never to die
(or we hope this for our family).

III.
We *can* "conquer" nature,
not by physical force, not by
trying to control or exploit her,
but by accepting God's full shelter.
Our soul can never be fulfilled
in illusion, forgetting the eternal,
pretending to be a king or a bug.

Our existence in matter seems
threatened, so we strive to achieve—
to "become" somebody—
again and again,
assuming different roles,
incurring karmic debt to pay back,
riding the never-ending Ferris wheel.

By blessings we become convinced
that matter's not our home.
The heart can't be satisfied
without achieving lasting love and wisdom.
Moved by an existential crisis,
we search out a guru

who inspires us, removes our doubts,
and gives us *sukriti* for Bhakti.

Bhakti, our highest potential,
brings us beyond misconception,
misery, death, and doubt
to the world of Krishna's service—
the spiritual world, Vrindavan—
a land of faith, the heart's homeland of giving.
There, the trees are service-fulfilling trees;
the water, nectar; speech, a song;
every step, a dance; and bliss, our nature.

Lord Chaitanya's Moon of the Holy Name Still Rises

I.
Over 500 years ago
in Nabadwip, West Bengal,
the lunar eclipse brought
the Hindus to Mother Ganga
to chant the holy names,
unknowingly heralding the appearance
of the *Yuga Avatar*
whose mission was to induce
everyone to chant *Hare Krishna*

in the ecstatic rapture of service and love.
In his *acharya lila,* Lord Chaitanya
demonstrated this practice.

II.
In a place far away
from Nabadwip, Chaitanya's influence
continues. He brought my guru,
Prabhupada, to awaken the forgetful,
empowering me for four decades
to keep the holy name
as my constant companion.
Despite my shortcomings,
my guru's mercy came to me,
personifying Shri Chaitanya
who gave Krishna's name
(with the highest pure love)
to the most destitute,
forlorn, discontented souls
made unhappy by materialism,
feeling incomplete
without the grace of Bhakti.

III.
Rising in early morning—
some would say
the middle of the night,
an "ungodly" hour—
I honor the hours before sunrise,
the yogic time of inner contemplation.
The *Gita* teaches us,

what is night for all
is the awakening time for yogis.
Or, one person's food is another's poison.
Our habits, faith, and attachments show
whom we hold dear,
what we strive for, and
where we will go at death
when all is revealed.

IV.
Preparing for temple service,
cleansing my body, dressing
in clean robes, painting my skin
with sacred clay *tilak* markings—
I remember Krishna, the proprietor
of my body and soul.
Then, I chant *Hare Krishna*
while I stoke the stove with dry tree bodies
to keep our Deities and their devotees warm.
Then I hop in the car,
hearing Krishna *katha* on the stereo.

V.
At the temple,
I unlock the doors, turn on the lights,
and offer obeisances to Prabhupada.
Singing the holy names,
I fetch the Deities' sweet
and flowers for *arati*.
Socks and shirt off,
a *harinama chader*

adorns my torso.
The holy names wake the Deities,
and I pray to awaken
my soul's identity in transcendental service.

VI.
Chanting mantras throughout the offering, I remember
my guru's mercy through *arati*,
the holy names always carrying me,
sustaining my life.
The Deities are bathed with water and—
guess what?
The holy names!
Fresh raiment and garlands
replace the old
while I pray for a spiritual body.

VII.
Then, the sounds of devotees
chanting *japa* on their tulasi rosaries,
meditating on the sacred sound
in the darkened temple room
while a recording of Prabhupada chanting *japa*
supports us in the background.
It's a blissful life each moment,
and we look forward to *Gaura Purnima*,
a celebration and festival inspiring us
to live by the holy name's mercy
for the rest of our lives and on into eternity.
Lord Chaitanya's moon is rising!
Let the holy name rise up in our hearts!

Beyond the Influence of the Stars

This is my first poem. I wrote it in the early 1980's.

This is the sojourn of an ignorant soul
looking for a real, satisfying role,
hoping to find the ultimate, final goal,
an end to suffering from illusion's toll.

At birth, in the stars a picture is taken,
revealing if we are blessed or perhaps forsaken.
A chart is plotted, the future told—
will we become ill, die young, or grow old?

Prestige and a mansion, along with fine sons,
a beautiful wife, and a bank full of funds—
or infamous, ugly, a pauper on the street,
no house of our own, no shoes on our feet.

Are we to be successful, have a good life,
or are we doomed to failure, suffering, and strife?
Achievement and lack we must understand
are deserved by us at God's command.

This is the sojourn of a bewildered soul,
absorbed in a false, temporary role,
not understanding the actual goal,
rebelling against the Lord's control.

On the path of life's destiny,
different pains and miseries—
this is a life of uncertainty,
a dualistic world of relativity.

Riches or fame, beauty or strength—
can life endure to the desired length?
When the material world is viewed all around,
can we avoid being put in the ground?

We don't want to die, fall ill, or grow old,
but hard as we try, no solution's been told!
Forced upon us, suffering is there,
but for the miseries of life, we don't really care.

The dilemma's not solved within matter's bounds,
but on the spiritual level, the answer is found.
Pleasure is lacking in a temporary state;
we're playing in a dream, not knowing our fate.

The body's a cage, a house in which we dwell;
the soul's a bird within a cell.
By cleaning the cage, the bird's not fed.
By starving the soul, we're as good as dead.

This is the sojourn of a confused soul,
unable to find a lasting role,
confined to relative, misleading goals,
forced to act under Maya's control.

The stars will show the future unfolding,
but thought is needed—worldly vision's withholding.
Beyond the stars' power is where we belong,
no grief or trouble, beyond the payment for wrongs.

The lesson to learn, it will be shown:
to discern matter from spirit—that's what's to be known.
We must consult a proper authority,
someone versed in *Vedic* thought and philosophy.

Complete knowledge is given by the *Vedas*,
written in Sanskrit on innumerable pages,
preserved from the minds of bygone ages,
told by the wise and learned sages.

Attentively hear this crucial information:
we're damned or blessed by reincarnation.
This truth is rarely actually seen;
we're blinded by hopes of enjoying the dream.

The soul is eternal, never slain.
Our enjoyment is only relief from pain.
We're used to chewing the chewed—
no satisfaction, yet it's forever pursued.

Nescience creates fear, not knowing God's will.
When the body dies, the soul lives on still.
This is knowledge, obtained after years.
In the Lord's kingdom, we're free from fears.

Tolerant of extremes, content with destiny—
then, and only then, will we reach tranquility.
The Lord is our shelter, protector, and dearest friend.
Loving him completely brings us to him in the end.

Our love is expressed by sharing his name,
from house to house we spread his fame.
He's the one we've been looking for—
our desires satisfied, no hankering anymore.

This is the end of the sojourn of a wise soul,
who found a real, satisfying role,
who attained the ultimate, final goal—
loving, and accepting God's control.

The Spiritual Basics Must Be Mastered (And It Takes a Long Time!)

I.
The basics revisited:
I write about it often—
simple spiritual life.
I know the theory by heart:
*We are spiritual beings
covered by body and mind.*
Oh, it seems old news.
I am such a mature devotee.

But truth be told,
realization is difficult.
It's a long education
of repeated trial and error—
the bare truth of embodiment
uncovered in the laboratory of life.
We need to hear it frequently,
think it over carefully.

So we practice: chanting
and contemplation, applying
the fundamentals in everyday activities—
in study and at work,
in marriage, with family and children—
doing what we must
with our desires and attachments,
adding what's most essential.
We practice remembering Krishna

at all times, in all places,
accepting what's helpful,
giving up what's not.
Seeing through the eyes of the scriptures,
the wise *sadhus*' words
present continual opportunities
to practice what we've learned.

II.
Blissful spring is here—
beautiful, but too short—
with so many duties.
As I pull weeds,
I think of unwanted plants.
They're like material desires
I once imagined I wanted
that now simply disturb.

We cause our own problems
on the quest for material joy.
But real happiness is from the soul,
not these covered senses—
we're feeling with a spacesuit on.
The body's such an inconvenience.
Material laws restrict and confine;
they promise greatly, but deliver minimally.

Our health totters, fails.
We lament our losses.
By aging, we diminish.
As I drive to the store, lessons:

"collateral damage," road kill—
a skunk or possum—spattered red glory.
There's a mangled deer to the side,
and later, the storeowner's cat with mange.

Two sides of the coin:
material misery/spiritual bliss.
Both can motivate us in Bhakti,
and the latter points to the former.
But we have to pray intently
to notice what life truly is:
spiritual practice is real life.
Our highest ideal carries us.

Prabhupada's Arrival in America

Today marks 50 years
since Prabhupada's arrival in America.
He was an emissary of Shri Chaitanya
as foretold by his chart at birth, predicting
he would travel overseas
to establish 108 temples.

Studying his life reveals
a lifetime of preparation:
kindling his fire of devotion,

realizing the scriptures,
learning practical knowledge with purity,
cultivating compassionate perseverance to save us.

The prediction of Shri Chaitanya—
that Krishna's holy name would spread
to every town throughout the world—
was thought by some to be a metaphor,
but Prabhupada believed it literally,
as did his guru who sent him to America.

As he prepared for his journey west,
obstacles appeared at every step,
difficulties that could defeat someone
less committed, yet he pushed forward tirelessly,
determined to succeed
with indomitable spiritual strength.

His future disciples were waiting
like dormant scattered seeds, not knowing
their destiny of Bhakti. Their lives were preparing them—
they were finding misery; they were searching for God.
Ultimately, they were fulfilled
only by Prabhupada's loving wisdom.

By the order of Prabhupada's guru,
we fallen souls were dispatched
to serve Prabhupada's mission
of spreading Krishna's holy name,
saving ourselves in the process
and passing the torch to others.

Prabhupada's example still inspires
his followers to continue serving,
awakening Bhakti within all.
Without Prabhupada's struggles,
none of us would know of Krishna
and we wouldn't find devotees in every land.

Prabhupada's glory will be fulfilled
when we all become pure devotees,
absorbed in unalloyed devotion,
sharing our good fortune
with no time for distractions,
giving kindness, compassion, and wisdom.

Ring Around the Rosie: We All Fall Down/Rise Up

Self-realization is a circle—
what goes up
must come down;
within the spring leaf,
the power to fall in autumn.
Vedic cosmology champions cyclical time.
Linear time's a modern illusion.
After the light—darkness,
begetting again the light.

Yesterday's gain
is today's forfeiture.

The TV season promises highly,
then reruns bore us.
Our favorite show, canceled.
Within our beloved life,
untimely death is born,
while the soul lives on,
covered by physical bodies.
Born again in hope;
lost again in time by design.
Terrestrial recycling:
dust to dust,
ashes to ashes,
earth to earth,
back to the future.

Life leaves clues
for the philosophical,
clues found by observing the moment.
We search and question,
prompted by the *Vedas*,
trusting that answers will come.
Sitting in the garden—
life's beautiful classroom—
simplicity reveals complexity.
As above, so below.
Watching the leaves descend
from sky to earth, changing
the landscape, the special ground covering

blown by the wind. The decaying leaf incense,
the crystal-clear, deep-blue sky,
the warm sun on my face—
big fall spiders wait patiently for
unsuspecting insects. Everyone has their time;
the universe is in the web.

The hidden foundation,
Source, and Supreme Cause
encourages our transformation—
conditioned souls, awaken!
Krishna sends his saints
and the scriptures, and our awareness
prompts spiritual remembrance.
Let go of earthly weights,
attachments, and worldly desires.
Let go of "happy" and "sad."
The holy name to the rescue!
He gives us wings to fly.
Krishna's arms await us
beyond the land of laws.
In the lawless land of love,
the spiritual plane of bliss,
there's unending joy, dance,
and song—our soul's hankering
awakened by a falling leaf.

Spiritual Variety in Universal Oneness

One Source, one Power—
and within oneness, diversity.
Shri Chaitanya's special gift:
everything one, yet different.
A distant, hazy mountain view
up close reveals form and variety.
One sun, infinite particles;
all-pervading Spirit Consciousness,
individual serving soul-units.

Beyond omnipresent light—
the formless, inconceivable Brahman—
is the realm of loving forms.
There, ecstasy takes a shape.
Variety and form promote taste.
Beyond a singular note,
there's a symphony of many voices.
Harmonic notes: one purpose,
united for shared love.

Disguised as servant and master,
there, all enjoy equally.
Beyond material duality,
no one lower or higher, everyone
gives selfless service.
One body, many cells;
one Truth in multiplicity.
Divine loving service unites—
Krishna is Love Supreme!

Without personal relationships—
the soul's relationship to Krishna,
Krishna's relationship to everyone and everything—
Govardhan puja would be self-worship. But
with proper understanding, in *Govardhan puja*
we celebrate cooperation
between nature, humanity, and divinity,
and highlight our joyful dependence,
the oneness of shared love.

By participating in regular spiritual practice, we learn to see through the eyes of scripture and to think spiritually, to perceive what's beyond the material dualities of good or bad, happy or sad. What might seem to others like an ordinary life of work, school, and family is a life full of meaning for a devotee of Krishna. We find lessons everywhere—if we are willing to look. Our ability to look for the seeds of instruction and mercy depends to a large extent on our positive absorption in thought and remembrance of Krishna. Our realization depends, in part, on our attitude toward life, what we seek, and where we give our energy. On the one hand, we see the shortcomings of matter everywhere, a life with no spirituality. We see how material attachments and desires slow our spiritual progress. On the other hand, we also see the arrangement of Krishna, how we are being guided and helped.

Though there are perhaps unlimited perceptions of life, in general we could say that there is a negative material perspective and a positive spiritual view. By this I don't mean to imply that difficult challenges or seemingly "bad" things don't happen to Krishna devotees. But, an advanced devotee always knows that behind the problematic situation there's an important lesson that may lead to more dependence on God. Depending on Krishna makes for a less stressful life, a life lived in increasing happiness and devotional advancement.

Everyone on the path of Bhakti knows that the goal of *Krishna prema* (love for Krishna) is the highest ideal. To the extent that we realize and act on this, we will experience deeper joy and even ecstatic moods in our spiritual practices. If our spiritual life seems stagnant or stuck, we can take note of what we are doing that doesn't foster our spiritual life. Then, we can increase or begin practices for becoming Krishna conscious. Our life can seem complex, and yet the solution to our problems is simple. We only need to believe in what's possible by the power of grace as we focus on the holy name and devotional service.

The following free-verse poem came to me as I contemplated the limitations of the material world, the root cause of all our suffering, and the ultimate spiritual solution.

Impurely Imitating, but Eventually Waking Up

Because we are part of God,
we have a similar nature—
comparable in quality, but very tiny.
The false ego covers this truth;
ignorance becomes our knowledge.
We become proud of borrowed plumes.
Forgetting Krishna, the body is everything.
An exploitive mentality rules and hides us,
a perversion of our spiritual serving nature.
We think our desires are who we are,
so we're willing to fight to protect what's "mine."
Pushing our body to the limit,
we try to recover with herbs and healers,
yet we're unable to defeat time's march.
Changing the body and mind restricts us
in the grip of death, disease, and old age.
Attempting to adjust material conditions,
we curse our suffering and limitations,
creating another body to try again.
We're on a never-ending physical battleground,
fighting with others for scarce resources,
repeatedly trying to enjoy matter.
But we're always defeated, put in our place,
until by grace, we gain a vision of truth
from a merciful saint giving the seed of Bhakti.
Lord Chaitanya has come to save us,
giving us the holy name, Vaishnava company,

devotional service, and relishable prasad.
We conquer the inner world
by taking shelter of Guru and Krishna.
Simple, it is, but very powerful
if we can give our heart and will.

Simple, Profound Truth

Sitting in the quiet sun room,
joyfully bright after dark days
of clouds, rain, and even a late frost
that killed leaves and plants too tender—
I watch the afternoon sun fading, the trees swaying gently,
and I think of our shared time together,
of trying to give you a good read,
wanting to attract the creative energy
of the citta, or reservoir of wisdom,
akin to Jung's collective unconscious mind.

Yet, I don't have to fabricate
extraordinary stories, events, and actions.
I only have to observe and remember,
praying to uncover the veiled message,
seeing nothing as ordinary or routine—
a frequent poem line, but true.
You can practice appreciation, too—

remember the wonder of a child.
We're only bored due to our distraction,
pumped up by modern culture's passion.

Driven by ever-increasing speed with no substance,
we're spoiled by convenience for no good reason
except to complicate life and create addiction.
We anticipate the next improved gadget,
yet feel empty with no soul food.
So we dull the numbness with intoxication.
Things seem to change, yet remain the same.
Some complain in vain without an alternative,
while a few are blessed with a spiritual solution,
an uplifting, lifetime goal—meaning for each moment.

Yesterday, a home Deity installation—
Shri Jagannath, Baladeva, and Subhadra:
special forms of God and his energy
blessings us with devotional opportunities.
We called the Lord to come by bathing them
with constant Hare Krishna kirtan.
Sitting in the homa, or sacred fire ceremony,
we called God into the fire, creating auspiciousness.
I prayed to him, asking him to burn up my sinful desires,
and bless me to serve by writing.

Offering grains, seeds, and my very soul,
in the here and now, I'm born yet again,
empowered to give, love, and help.
I'm grateful in blissful devotee company, satisfied
with simple, yet profound devotional activities,

full of deep meaning and philosophy,
yet powered by love and devotion.
We pray to uncover our heart and soul,
to increase our spiritual aspirations
and understand what's truly essential.

---

*If you have built castles in the air,
your work need not be lost;
that is where they should be.
Now put foundations
under them.*
Henry David Thoreau

God gave burdens, also shoulders.
Yiddish Proverb

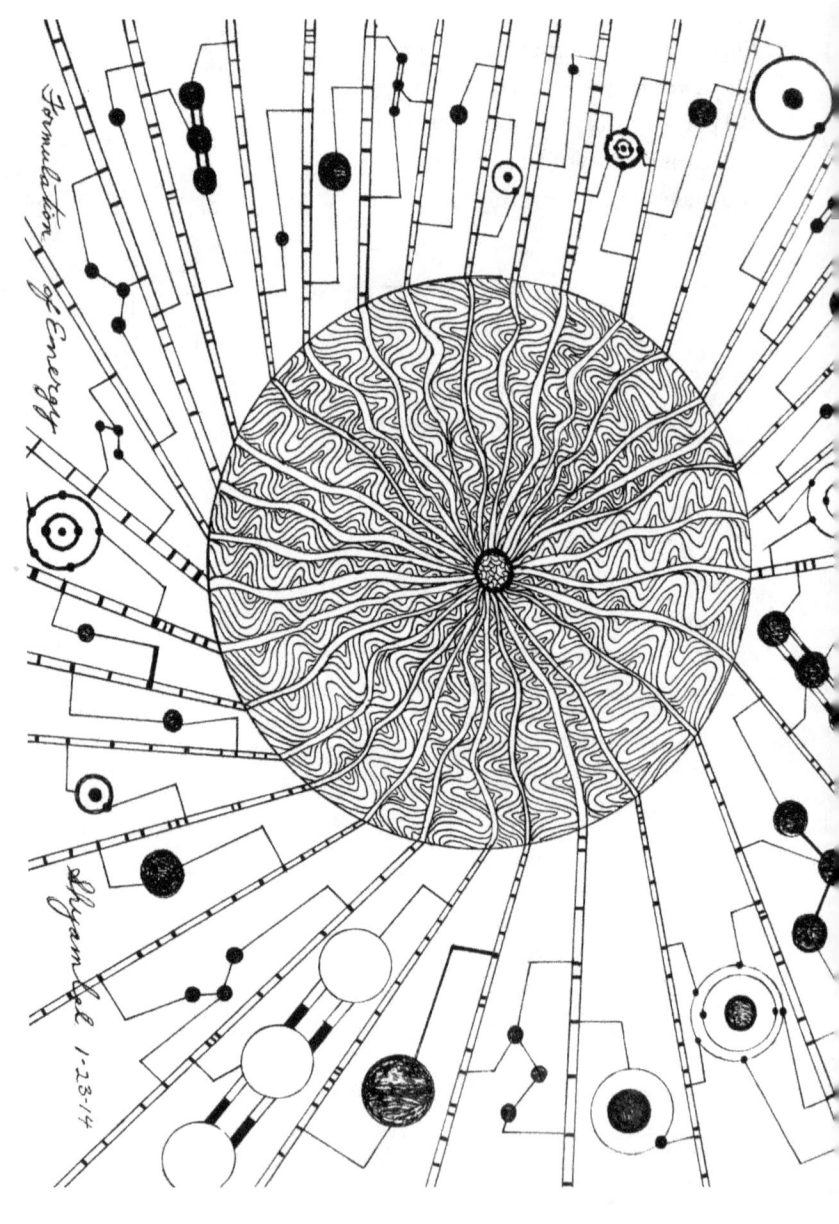

Chapter 5

LIVING FULLY

In Endymion, I leaped headlong into the sea, and thereby have become better acquainted with the soundings, the quicksands, and the rocks, than if I had stayed upon the green shore, and piped a silly pipe, and took tea and comfortable advice.
John Keats

Affirmation of life is the spiritual act by which man ceases to live unreflectively and begins to devote himself to his life with reverence in order to raise it to its true value. To affirm life is to deepen, to make more inward, and to exalt the will to live.
Albert Schweitzer

*Ships are safe remaining in protected harbors,
but that's not what ships are built for.*
attributed to various people with various wording,
but true regardless

Becoming More by Working at Kindred Spirits

Working is a mixed blessing,
giving up retirement
and honoring my need
to be with others.

People bring me joy
and fulfill my purpose to give.
I like meeting spiritual seekers
or just normal shoppers,

sharing hope and encouragement,
giving kindness with useful wisdom
and simultaneously earning a paycheck.
It's a celebration of giving and receiving—a win/win.

The energy of money
represents freedom,
helps me to thrive
instead of just survive.

Yet, I am busier
than I would like,
which makes life
whoosh by so fast.

Usually, we have either
time or money,
rarely both,
though it's possible.

I am contemplating
this delicate balance,
grateful for
my life opportunities.

The struggle is good—
I'm forced not to stagnate
because I must stretch
to realize my highest potential.

My Life's Creed

What's yours?

I.
Opening an inner portal,
I find my conscious awareness
of being, opening
to receive and share truth.

My soul radiates
love and blessings,
my need to connect deeply
with others in lasting friendship.

Sorting out my psychology
from my soul's identity has been

a very long study, using introspection,
third-person perspective, spiritual practice, and prayer.

My soul—the real me—
remains entwined with body and mind,
funneling spiritual necessities
though my conditioned identity.

I have such an intense need
to really understand myself,
how my karmic body limits me
while hinting at transcendence.

Oh, the intensity to share
my journey with you in a personal way,
without pretense or profile, not always PC,
but hopefully useful to some.

The universal desire to be loved
and understood by those who love
and understand us, the desire for total oneness,
the desire to become one soul in many bodies—

it's a very strong desire, a yearning
caused in part by insecurity. In me, it comes from
the fear of abandonment I felt as a child.
But everyone's hidden desire is union with God.

Important to my inner work—
I uncovered two primal necessities:

I want to be free, and, *I want
to be real.* These urges so move me!

This fuels my search for those
with whom I can exchange
in total honesty and love
while endeavoring to be freed from earthly bonds.

II.
The material world is the plane
of bondage, limitation, and imposed conditions
that seem to require overcoming, creating
the constant struggle to become full and satisfied.

I do understand this on a deep level
from the experience of many births and of yoga,
yet my attachment to matter prevents me
 from totally embracing my Supreme Beloved.

I have been searching for my Beloved
through eternity—I'm an old soul—
which means I'm a slow learner,
existing as a human being for way too long.

So now I share with you my frustrations
and struggles, along with my spiritual success.
While enjoying the same old worldly stuff,
I keep endeavoring for spiritual perfection.

Spiritual perfection involves realizing
our soul beyond the body and

fulfilling its true primal hankering by loving
Krishna in eternal serving consciousness.

In our eternal consciousness as a soul,
we have no material needs or conditioning,
and we love our Supreme Beloved, which includes
everyone and everything. We only serve, give, and share

with Radha and Krishna, with no self-interest.
Egotistical self-interest only arises from mistaken
identification with matter. But realizing our Self as part
of the Supreme, we can't help but act for the Supreme interest.

We are one with God in purpose and heart,
yet we're an individual unit.
of serving consciousness. So in serving
the Supreme interest, we nurture and serve our real Self.

I will arrive "there" someday, when
I perceive the world as a facility for service,
when I see selfishness as unimaginable,
when my heart and soul are given to Krishna.

Spiritual progress is a gradual process through
many forms of giving to others and Krishna. We're encouraged
by chanting mantras in japa and group singing,
by associating with saints, and endeavoring for pure love.

Putting Bhakti, love, into everything I do,
I look for opportunities to serve and give to others—

ultimately for their spiritual benefit—
giving in any way I can with prayerful well-wishing.

Divine Change Agent

Presenting a snapshot, a picture,
I share where I often dwell:
in contemplation of this life
and my real spiritual nature.

We are all so complex—
if we really dig deep,
beyond superficial lies,
parts of many births color us.

Just because I live, yearning,
my heart beats. I feel
amidst objects and things—temporal matter.
A diamond cage imprisons, saddens.

In the body, we're projecting
our desires, projecting our "my"
onto our made-up "I"—
the ego's delight; the soul's plight.

Thank God, the holy name unravels
illusory desires, giving a higher taste.
Still, my life is swirling between
these subtle dimensions.

Our soul's nature is to serve,
but the question is: *Whom or what should we serve?*
Our senses? Our heart? Our mind? Or
the Lord of Love, flute-playing Krishna? Our choice.

Oh, will you save me
from myself by allowing
my real self—who is yours—
to emerge from under so many layers?

Sitting in Kindred Spirits, feeling
the music, I'm thinking of you amidst
the glamour of jewels, delicious smells,
delightful colors—symbols of all religious traditions.

I'm a tiny giver—who
can I really help? At least myself?
I help some partially, while others are repelled.
Still, I pray for them.

Every moment is an opportunity
to give, share, and love more—
regardless of our occupation,
we can be a divine change agent!

Spiritual life is about change—
shedding our temporary skin,
remembering who we truly are
and giving remembrance to others, like a light.

To the degree our soul is
uncovered, selfishness is lost.
When the Lord is the goal of our heart,
we can be helpful to our self and others.

Tomorrow is created by today. It begins today.
So many todays make months and years
of life—then the death of our body
brings our final exam for this life.

And so I live and choose—since each day is
all I have and I may die today or tomorrow—
to love and serve (After all, what is valuable?)
more today than yesterday.

Most of my poems were originally written for those involved or interested in *Gaudiya Vaishnavism*, and that is likely my main audience. Still, reading these poems now, thinking about a broader readership, I can see how this poem and others might seem sectarian. It might sound like I want to convert everyone to my way of thinking. I like my path, for sure, yet no path is for everyone. In general, I do recommend that everyone take a spiritual journey and believe in a higher power. That is my bias based on experience, and yet I still encourage everyone to follow their convictions while remaining open to other possibilities. Then, we can all learn and grow and come to understand that there is so much beyond our perception.

The spiritual worldview offers just as many convincing arguments for the devout as atheism offers for the adherents of the materialist understanding. From the perspective of reincarnation, everyone has a pre-existing proclivity for attraction to a particular path and its unique reasoning. Actually, the soul and God are trans-rational, beyond the mind and intellect, so it is no wonder that the divine dimension can seem like a great mystery.

On Preparing for Death While Living Fully

As a youth, and even as a young devotee,
I never really thought about my death,
strange as that may seem.
I was insulated, living in a college town
with no relationship to anyone who died.
Living with and noticing only the young,
I didn't realize that every day is a gift.
Though I spoke that to others, it was only a theory.

I have learned that hearing from scripture provides
the best evidence of material life's shortcomings. Yet,

we need experience to get our attention. We need
the trial of life's fiery ordeal, or others' grief.
Personal setbacks, diseases, difficulties, and death catapult us
beyond the conditioned tendency, beyond the belief that
life and health are our birthright. Our faculties can be withdrawn at any moment, but we're blind to this.

Knowing I am eternal, without birth or death,
is very helpful for living peacefully.
It helps me remain fixed on the straight and narrow,
praying to always remember Guru and Krishna.
Yet, aging and death are still disconcerting.
So many people I have known
have become ill and have left their bodies behind.
Every day my physical demise is closer.

As an aspiring Bhakta, my shelter is Krishna,
his holy name, scripture, and Deity service.
I aspire for the company of truly advanced devotees,
yet in some ways I'm also a typical human being—
I want appreciation, and I want to benefit others materially,
to leave behind a contribution, a legacy,
even though nothing material lasts.
But service to devotees endures, as it pleases Krishna.

Ordinary people think that living fully means
living with maximum stimulation and sense enjoyment,
living through fascinating experiences
and unlimited entertaining diversions.
They glorify the act of helping others to do the same.
This is night for a real devotee,

who aspires to be absorbed in the holy name,
in hearing, chanting, and remembering *Radha-Krishna lila*.

How much conviction do I have
that worldly facilities provide no real hope
for lasting happiness and fulfillment?
How do I act upon the knowledge
of matter's temporality and lessening returns?
My true focus is the bliss of
serving the Lord of my heart
along with his devotees in full love.

Personally, I have enough understanding
to invest my remaining years in divine practice,
fueled by my realization that I live on spiritually
by Krishna's kindness and arrangement.
I meditate: every step, every breath, every thought,
every written word is mercy. My life,
though imperfect, is only his. It is to be offered in service
to my gurus and to whomever Krishna desires me to help.

High aspirations and steady practice
are essential for my spiritual progress.
Lord Chaitanya doesn't see our past
or present failures, but only our heartfelt ideal.
His mercy will impel us to know the superlative nature
of our ultimate goal—*Krishna prema*—why
it is so much better than materialism. His mercy will keep us
on the path, inspiring us to prayerfully cry for success.

To Begin Coming to Krishna: How Much Faith Is Enough?

I.
Someone asked me,
*How much faith is enough
to stay on the path?*
Hmm . . . 5%, 20%, 50%, 100%?
Is knowing one or two parts of
essential truth enough,
or is it all or nothing?
How much faith is required
to try something new—
to drive, fly, or walk in the dark?

Many experienced something
otherworldly in my guru, Prabhupada—
his character, wisdom, and kindness
charmed our hearts and touched us deeply.
Our love and service flowed to him greatly!
We served him tirelessly, wanting to please him
and make him smile. Thus, we were happy,
having faith and inspiration to continue,
never thinking it would end.

Without knowing the words, I experienced
that faith in Krishna and his representative
is more than daydreaming or mental belief.
Our faith in him and experience of Bhakti
let us accept the goal of *prema*,
allowed us to have faith in the unseen and inconceivable.

The spiritual world is the land of faith,
upliftment, song, dance, and bliss;
the material world is the land of doubt,
delusion, death, disease, and misery.
We already knew this; now it was confirmed.

Devotees of Krishna
have various levels of faith,
realization, and experience,
compelling them to dedicate
much of their lives to pursuing
the ideal of *Krishna prema,*
even while material desires and
attachments to worldly things remain.

Who can take up Bhakti?
Anyone who truly wants it,
having received blessings
from pure devotees,
present, past, or future.

From Prabhupada, I received
a superlative gift: faith
in spiritual obtainment,
the feeling of heart fulfillment.
As my life unraveled
in answer to my inner call,
I responded to the intensity
of my dormant longing for Krishna,
which amazed and compelled
this formerly dull person.

II.
How could I so easily give up
my material possessions,
my prospects for a "happy" life—
my girlfriend, my "security,"
my education, my career path—
to live as an ashram monk?
A material, plausible explanation
could be given: my alcoholic familial environment,
the influence of the 60's counterculture movement.
Yet, the *Gita* tells us this was all arranged
to foster a revival of my dormant attraction
to Krishna, which began in past lives
with faith in yoga and the holy name.

Bhakti is potentially good for all,
yet few are interested.
We must have great necessity
to remain on the path
or even try the path on for size,
see if it fits or if we can grow into it
by practice, becoming an essence seeker.

You may have to separate
spiritual consciousness from imitation
or fanatical presentations.
You will have to gain experience
of Krishna by chanting, seeking
good spiritual association, serving Deities,
and eating spiritualized food called *prasad*.

Service is the real solace and
the means for purification!

A little spiritual experience of
Krishna's mercy or presence
is more powerful than any material satisfaction —
education, wealth, worldly reputation —
it all pales before a drop of Krishna's mercy.
I'm living proof of this reality,
along with many other practitioners.

Yet, until you have experience,
nothing will convince you completely.
Your heart will remain doubtful,
uncommitted. You'll stay
on the outside licking the honey jar.

III.
Souls can achieve their desires,
either in matter or spirit,
so if you like the ideal and philosophy
of Bhakti but remain unable
to take it up, pray intensely
for divine assistance and faith,
for experiential confirmation
that this is your path, or not.
A drop of faith is more powerful
than an ocean of doubt.
By humility, you will realize
that neither material qualifications

nor intelligence will help you
come to love Krishna.

Find those Bhakti yogis
who inspire you and
embody spirituality; serve them in joy.
Purification comes through
service, which removes
Maya's veil of illusion and allows
the soul's wisdom to shine.
Take the medicine of the holy name,
the supreme prayer
to obtain Krishna's grace.
Krishna is present in his
name and service;
wherever devotees glorify him,
he resides in their hearts.

My bias: the charming beauty of Krishna,
the ideal of Shri Chaitanya—
I embrace this as my
North Star. For me,
no philosophy can compare
to the sweetness of sharing Krishna
with others, the bliss of *kirtan*,
and the reciprocation of the Deities.
It's all more than I deserve,
and it makes me smile
as I feel it in wonder!

This is a whole way of life,
which at some point becomes
an identity. The best way to live:
chanting three hours a day for 45 years
with many ups and downs,
better today than yesterday,
celebrating life and Krishna's appearance days
or those of his saintly devotees.
I find nothing else to do
that brings me lasting happiness.

If you knew me at 18 and now at 65,
you would understand my evolvement,
how Bhakti transforms. Sometimes slowly, painfully,
leaving rough, unfinished edges for much too long.
Yet, gradually, surely, Bhakti polishes everything.
I know Krishna is not through with me.
I will drown in the ocean of ecstatic bliss—
today, tomorrow, in some lifetime—
this I know for certain by faith and experience!

Living and Dying for Krishna: Emperor Parikchit's Example

Emperor Parikchit of *Bhagavat* fame
was a first class devotee, a king
of wonderful birth. He lived
a glorious life of service, and he died
an auspicious, exemplary death.
He's a worthy person
about whom spiritual seekers
can inquire and hear.

An amazing leader with kingly opulence,
he increased the Pandu dynasty's prestige.
He appeared to have everything.
Why, then, did he renounce the world
to sit on the bank of the Ganges?
What did he wish to learn
at the time of his impending death?

Such a powerful ruler,
his enemies bowed to him,
surrendering their wealth
to receive his blessings.
He was full of youth, strength, and
unsurpassed wealth.
How could he give up everything,
even his very life?

Great souls devoted to the Lord's cause
live only to help others

without personal benefit. Emperor Parikchit was free
from any worldly attachment.
So why did he need to renounce his life
when his body sheltered others?

Such questions are excellent and glorious
as they're related to Shri Krishna
and his devotees. Beneficial to all,
elevating material consciousness,
spiritual inquiry contrasts with ordinary talk
that perpetuates birth, death, and misery.

Having been cursed for a minor offense,
King Parikchit joyfully accepted his lot,
thinking himself an offender
and seeing that Krishna's mercy would
disentangle him. He saw an opportunity
for perfection by saintly association,
his mind absorbed in Krishna!

For our benefit, Krishna arranged
the curse so Shukadeva could speak,
so Parikchit could inquire,
and so all could hear about Krishna,
whose pastimes destroy materialistic life
and give a higher taste that matures
into *Krishna prema*, pure love.

Krishna with his devotees did their part
to exemplify and teach the ideal.
Now it's our responsibility and opportunity

to use time properly by hearing and chanting,
living our lives by the *Bhagavat* philosophy.

What Is Life About? Where Is Happiness?

What is life about?
From one perspective,
life is what you make it.
It's what you want
and what you're able to get.

Another way of saying this:
you have inclinations,
you endeavor, and you have success
or failure in making your desires manifest.
Some may call this your destiny.

Why do you want
what you want?
There are two levels,
two reasons for this—
one primary and primal,
the other secondary,
and, truth be told, illusory.

Why illusory?
Because our spiritual nature is

our real, eternal identity. We are souls,
units of consciousness that radiate
our true, original nature—
our desire to serve and give to the Center.
Right now, we're covered by a material body
with senses, and we're led by their attractions.

We are trying in vain
to satisfy our spiritual hankering
through our physical body and mind.
We repeatedly take birth and die,
trying to be successful
in so many species, on so many planets.

It's like we're cleaning the cage of a bird
but forgetting the bird needs food.
It can only live and thrive
if it's fed; otherwise, it's dead.
We can live forever
when we find our spiritual food.

Real life is eternal life;
true happiness is lasting happiness;
factual identity is the soul.
What's generally considered the self
is actually karmic desires based on the senses,
whatever we materially want and earn.

When you look in the mirror
or at someone else,

you're seeing consequences
of previous actions. Karma and reincarnation
aren't fatalistic; they're crystallized justice
teaching everyone that we're the architects
of our own fortune or misfortune,
facilitated by the laws of God.

Cause and effect are God's laws,
meant to reform us and
point to the Law Maker,
to direct us toward our spiritual identity,
our loving relationship with
the Supreme Powerful, our Source,
the ultimate Cause of all causes.

Beyond this, more importantly,
he is our dear-most friend,
our well-wisher, and the love of our life.
Everything else is a way to hide from this truth
by putting ourselves in the center
rather than accepting
we're only part of the Center.

We are meant to revolve around that Center
like loving friends, cooperating to serve
our mutual interest, discovering our true, lasting happiness
in this life and forever, becoming free at last,
coming home to our blissful residence
where we never leave our heart's satisfaction.

Neither Here Nor There—
So, Where Are You?

On the road from New Vrindavan to home,
a refreshing highway rest stop in West Virginia
sits at the bottom of a ravine. Sharp, steep slopes
covered by trees are decorated above by a deep, blue sky.
Lazy, puffy clouds contrast with the highway's fast pace.
I sit with my wife honoring our *Krishna prasad* lunch,
observing harried motorists park and move to the bathroom.
A smile is rare, and they seem neither here nor there,
disconnected from the moment, unaware of life's beauty.

Observing all varieties of cars coming and going
with their precious cargo of souls covered by desires
displayed in a variety of physiques and dispositions,
I marvel at such bodily gifts bestowed to wayward souls
who all seek pleasure, friendship, and harmony.
I have unity with everyone as a human and soul,
though I'm surprised to see so many still smoking,
which can't satisfy the soul's yearning for fulfillment,
so I wonder how to help sleeping souls awaken.

No one seems to notice the "ordinary" workers
who clean the bathrooms, empty the garbage,
and keep the facilities in order to assist our travel.
So, as I dispose of my plate, I smile and speak
to a worker as she empties the trash.
She looks like a different person—

her face lights up—and when I see her again
she beams, wishing me a good day.
A little appreciation and kindness go far!

Rather than merely trying to get somewhere,
waiting for something significant to happen,
filling our lives with handheld distractions,
we can practice being present in the moment,
observing our surroundings and the people we encounter.
Life isn't in the future, but in the eternal now.
(Yes, we've all heard this, so I'm reminding us.)
Even if you are standing in a slow line,
share your heart, practice patience, and smile.
Be grateful to observe the spirit of the moment.

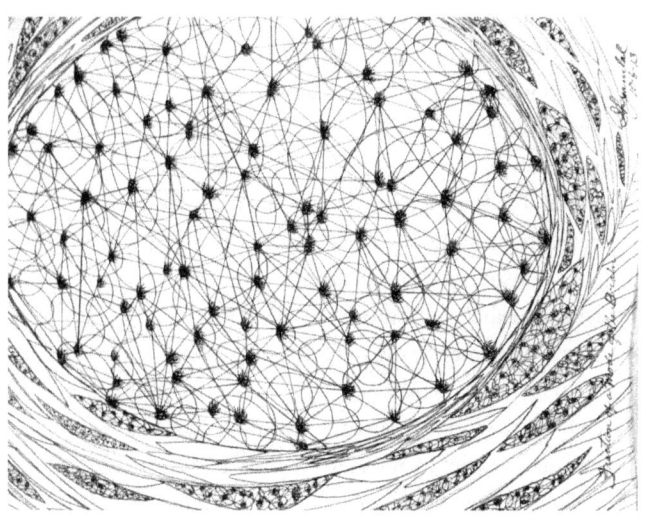

Saved from Cosmic Crud

Remembering my material sojourn:
I'm caught up in the waves of a cosmic storm
of ever-increasing change and uncertainty—
swirling, frightening energy moving @ mind speed,
lightning and wind amidst thunderous explosions.
Bewildered, pulled in all directions, but move nowhere.
I'm desperate for stability, fulfillment, truth, and peace—
a lasting resting place with loving feelings.
I want to understand who I really am, through and through,
to know my relationship to life and the universe.
I'm searching to find meaning in chaos and misery.

But, as soon as I get comfortable and settled,
I morph into a karmic soccer ball, mercilessly kicked
up and down the universal field into the goalposts of duality.
I'm spun in a misery-go-round at warp speed
and repeatedly cast out into an endless sea,
then I'm washed up on the shore of mediocrity.
Grabbed, I'm kneaded into gooey cosmic dough,
ingredients for someone else's manna.
I'm fried on an open fire and the leftovers become my body.
Emerging, exhausted, into an edible landscape,
hungry beings pursue me with dripping lips and angry eyes.

With bleeding wounds, I barely avoid being eaten.
From one calamity to another, *How can I continue?*
Then, out of nowhere comes a helping hand.
The light of truth beckons me forward.
Among nature's rhythm in celestial forests,

the red sky trees call me to learn by opening my heart.
Everything vibrates to divine musical scores.
The hidden Composer gives clues, prompts his seers.
He sends his secret agents who joyfully embody mercy.
Krishna's flute song is music's source and purpose,
made available through his penetrating holy names.

Hearing the transcendental sound
vibrated by pure, dancing devotees with loving eyes,
my past rolls up in the palm of my hand. The meaninglessness
of vain people and their confusing, sticky matrix falls away.
My old karmic residue gradually disintegrates.
The veneer of youthful beauty smells repulsive,
but old habits die hard; they fight to endure.
So, I still have to choose at every moment
whether to serve illusion or the real Lord of my heart.
I choose Krishna by serving with taste, loving him
by the mercy of Shri Guru, Gauranga, and the *Vaishnava*s.

The Day the Sun Didn't Rise

Today, the sun didn't rise.
I kept waiting, perplexed.
The wind howled.
Rain came in sheets.
Electric power failed.

No machines worked,
not even computers.
I lit candles, ancient technology.
Our Deities illuminated
on the altar again, I prayed,
Oh Lord, what is going on?
Going upstairs, I found my wife
had vanished. *Such things can't be happening!*

I felt afraid, uncertain.
Putting on my rain suit,
I noticed the falling temperature.
The front door flew open;
water wetted the walls.
I ventured outside,
struggling with all my might
to shut the door behind me.
My flashlight hardly worked
and dense fog surrounded me.
I had almost zero visibility.
I moved slowly against the gale to find
my car was gone!

I heard the sound of snapping branches
and a tree fell before me,
blocking my path.
Startled, my heart pounded
and I changed course,
walking on slowly. Finally,
I reached the house
of my neighbors, who are always home.

But, no cars were in the driveway.
I keep knocking with no answer until
the wind blew open the door,
revealing empty rooms—no furniture inside.
The stale smell of mildew accosted me.

Some four-legged creature approached.
A dog? No, a huge rat!
A python wrapped him up.
Bewildered, I couldn't believe
this was happening. *I must be dreaming.*
Gaining composure, I thought:
Day dream or night dream,
both are the same.
Coming and going,
always changing,
only the soul lasts
as part of eternal Krishna:
Hare Krishna, Hare Krishna.

I finally remembered to chant.
Difficulty reveals our faith.
We see our fears and attachments.
Introspection is a blessing,
a chance to own our shadow,
a chance to find the root
of our spiritual hesitancy
and pray to work through it.
Finding my real strength,
I headed back to the house,
fighting the wind and rain,

the sound deafening.
Every step was hard won.

I couldn't believe the struggle
just to walk and keep going.
We take for granted what's "ordinary"
until we don't have it.
Finally, I saw our home.
After entering I struggled
to close the door.
The Deities shone splendidly,
a reassuring presence
amidst the unpredictable,
uncertain world.
Removing my wet clothes,
I dried and re-dressed.

Grabbing my *japa* beads,
I sat before our merciful Lords.
Sitting there, I felt
unbelievable bliss. Although
I don't understand the events
in my life, it doesn't matter.
I can always take shelter
of the holy name
and pray for mercy.
When all else fails,
Krishna's love remains.
He always helps us
see what's really important.

Deck-Mates—Tiny Construction Instruments Try to Remember Krishna

During a busy week, I gradually put together the following poem documenting some of my thoughts during the construction of a deck.

Accomplishing even the smallest task
requires assistants, facilities, and prerequisites—
both seen and unseen. Past karma, current desires—
so many subtle pillars give support.
The *Gita* teaches that there are five factors of action—
each component essential for accomplishment—
and only one is the actual endeavor! Understanding this requires a philosophical and spiritual outlook,
since today, endeavor and luck are thought supreme.
Keeping this in mind, my son and I build a deck,
praying to remember Krishna and to offer the work to him.

Time is one factor of action:
my son's layoff from work gave him time.
With available money, we bought the materials.
Someone cut the trees and cured and shaped the wood.
Minerals were mined to make metals fashioned into tools.
Machines and fasteners were used at every step:
drills, screws, bolts, nails, and saws. Vehicles and bodies,
powered by oil, gas, electricity, and sweat,
transported the materials to the store
and delivered them across the miles to our country door.

Life's most essential ingredient is God,
who pervades all things, is everything.
Like the sun, sun-rays, and sun deity,
God sustains the universe—he *is* the universe.
Individual souls animate matter,
continuing its purposeful existence by karma.
Fueled by desires to enjoy, matter provides bodies.
Universal laws give facilities within limitations.
Ordained by God, we have our tiny independence.
Yet, special care is given to the godly,
those who want to serve, not exploit.
We pray to be counted as Krishna's devotees!

After a week of 100-degree weather,
torrential rains come and go.
We work between the storms,
feeling purposeful, yet insignificant.
We experience the roaring, crashing
force of the thundershower's power,
which also flows through our veins
and keeps our hearts beating, our eyes seeing,
our minds planning
(and wondering about God's greatness)
our arms carrying loads, and our hands grasping tools.
From the deck's foundation up: growing energy.
Each step builds on the previous
until the deck is complete and usable.
It looks as if it has always been there, permanent.
It teaches us how everything is manifested.

We complete the day's work
and clean up as darkness falls.
The final storm of the day approaches,
coming closer and growing louder each moment.
It brings everything to a stop and we run inside
as our attention goes upward to the spectacle:
lightning and thunder, simultaneous at times,
shaking the house with huge explosions.
Trees move wildly in a celestial rave.
Raindrops reverberate in surround sound like machine guns.
Whether we live or die, may we take Krishna's shelter,
knowing we exist and breathe only by his mercy,
praying to do our duties for him, accepting life events,
remembering his *lila* and his presence in our experiences,
adding the holy name to our throats and hearts.
Our only independence, and joy, is to depend on Krishna.

A Lotus in the Redwoods

A summary of the beginning of my spiritual journey:
Pensive on a mountaintop,
looking through modern civilization
almost covered by smog,
I'm adrift in a sea of uncertainty—
atomic threats and toxic chemicals.
No charted course appeals.
The answers provided are shallow;

all paths appear pointless.
Unlimited choices dull the brain.
Walking among the living dead,
I see complacency dressed as a virtue;
the status quo bewilders me.
Worldly recommendations disappoint.
Sensual thoughts and desires frustrate;
dogs chase their tails repeatedly.
I see a world of smashed dreams, vain hopes.

In the midst of random chaos—
calamities surrounding me,
indifference threatening my survival—
out of my bleeding heart,
a lotus in the redwood forest
reveals a divine purpose.
Now covered by madness,
nature's order reveals the law,
a reason for doing and being
beyond the fast track to dying.
Yet, death impels the wise
on the path of lasting truth—
the secret of joyous living—
awakening the mystic journey,
the meaning in misery
that leads to the soul's home.

A hidden force guides me,
a script long ago decided.
The spiritual path emerges
when all other doors close.

Krishna's holy name empowers:
ten thousand lasers drill,
cracking miles of concrete illusion,
allowing the soul to shine.
Blessed by gurus and sages,
I'm forced to surrender, then I choose.
Whether going forward or becoming lost again,
I stay in Krishna's embrace.
He carries my lack
and preserves my progress.
Everything serves the goal,
the quest of divine love.

Appendices

The Supreme Lord is not obtained by expert explanations,
by vast intelligence, or even by much hearing.
He is obtained only by one whom he himself chooses.
To such a person, he manifests his own form.
Mundaka Upanisad, 3.2.3

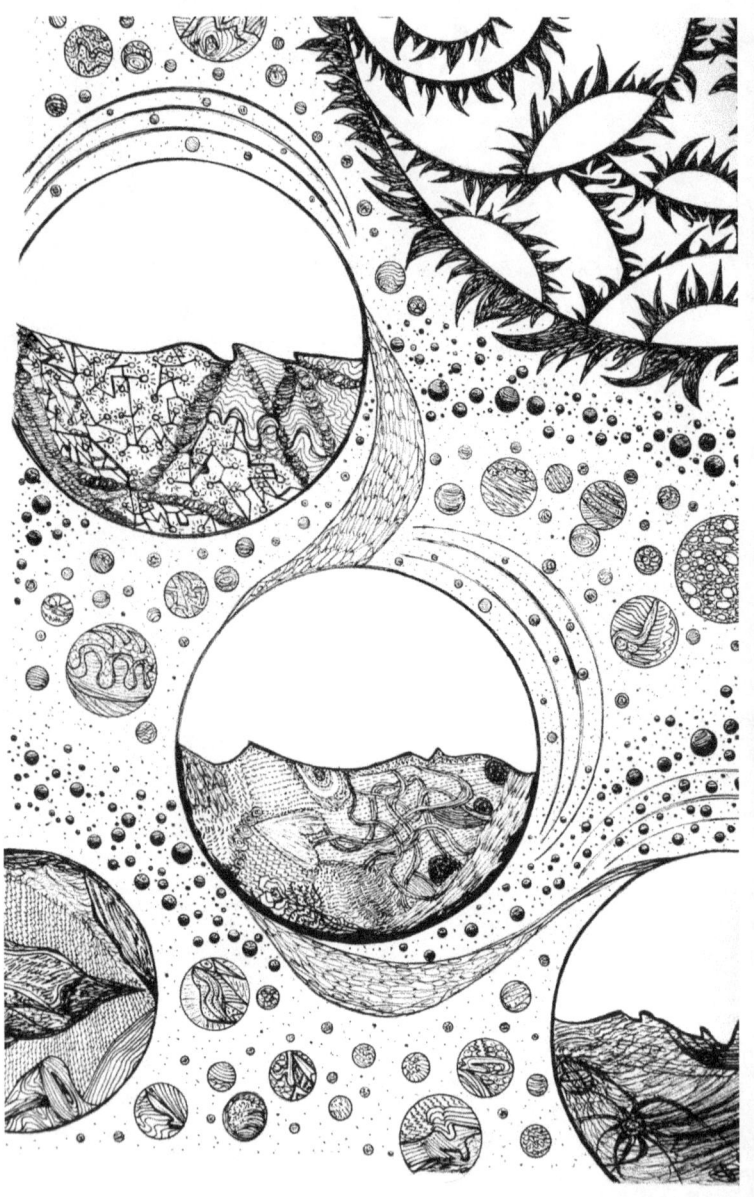

GLOSSARY

I have not used the scholarly system of transliteration of Sanskrit terms because most people are not familiar with this system and I'm attempting to make this book as user-friendly as possible. Rather, I've rendered Sanskrit terms phonetically so that English-speaking readers can pronounce unfamiliar terms according to the rules of speech they already know.

Acharya: one who teaches by his example, a spiritual master, though generally used for very prominent ones.

Acharya-lila: Lord Chaitanya's life in the role or pastime (*lila*) of a teacher (*acharya*).

Ashram (a): 1) one of the four spiritual orders of life: *Brahmachari*, student life; *grihastha*, married life; *vanaprastha*, retired life; or *sannyasa*, the renounced order of life. 2) *Ashram* also refers to the home of the spiritual master, or any place where spiritual practices are executed. A spiritually-minded couple may call their home their ashram, as their primary interest is spiritual cultivation—a very welcome perspective.

Bhagavad Gita: also called *Gitopanishad*, is roughly translated as *The Song of God*. It is a dialog between Krishna and Arjuna from one chapter of the *Mahabharata* epic. Although it is considered the ABCs of spiritual life, it contains everything a person needs for spiritual perfection, provided one hears its message from a bona fide guru coming in disciplic succession from Lord Chaitanya and his followers.

Bhakti (yoga): the system of cultivation of pure devotional service, which is untinged by sense gratification or philosophical speculation; the process of devotional service to the Supreme Personality of Godhead, Lord Krishna, consisting of nine *angas*, or parts: 1) hearing and 2) chanting about the transcendental holy name, form, qualities, paraphernalia, and pastimes of Lord Krishna, 3) remembering them, 4) serving the lotus feet of the Lord, 5) offering the Deity form of the Lord respectful worship with sixteen types of paraphernalia, 6) offering prayers to the Lord, 7) serving his mission, 8) making friends with the Lord, and 9) surrendering everything unto him (in other words, serving him with the body, mind, and words). These nine processes are accepted as pure devotional service.

Brahma: the empowered *deva* (higher being, archangel, or demigod) called the "creator," who is better described as an engineer since nothing is created, but only manifest or unmanifest before our vision.

Brahman or Brahmajyoti: the impersonal bodily effulgence emanating from the transcendental body of the Supreme Lord, Krishna, which constitutes the brilliant illumination of the spiritual sky. From Krishna's transcendental personal form of eternity, knowledge, and bliss emanates a shining effulgence called the Brahmajyoti (light of Brahman, clear Light). For many mystics and philosophers the world over, the Brahmajyoti is the indefinable One from which all things emerge in the beginning and into which all things merge at the end. This all-pervading light is Krishna's feature of *sat* (eternality), separated from *cit* (knowledge) and *ananda* (bliss).

(Lord) Chaitanya (Mahaprabhu): (also called Gaura, Gaura-Hari, and Gauranga) Lord Krishna's incarnation in the Age of Kali, who comes in the mood and complexion of his greatest devotee, Shri Radha. He appeared in Nabadwip, West Bengal in the late fifteenth century and inaugurated the *yuga-dharma* (prime religious process for the age): the congregational chanting of the divine names of God. He taught the highest goal of worshiping Krishna (God) in pure, materially unmotivated love, or *prema*.

Chanting Hare Krishna or other holy names of God: praising and glorifying God, surrendering ones total being to his will. Chanting is praying, giving thanks for life while seeing oneself as Krishna's servant. It is remembering, meditating on, and associating with God, since he is present in his names.

Devotee: Aside from the general dictionary meaning, it is specifically used in *Gaudiya Vaishnavism* as a brief way to designate a practitioner of Bhakti devoted to Krishna, or a practitioner of *shuddha-Bhakti* (pure loving devotional service to Krishna) as outlined in *Bhagavad Gita*, *Shrimad Bhagavatam*, *Chaitanya Charitamrita* and other devotional *Vedic* scriptures.

Diksha: the spiritual initiation of a disciple by a spiritual master into *Gaudiya Vaishnava* spiritual practices, such as chanting the *Gayatri mantra*.

Diksha guru: a guru who gives spiritual initiation.

Ganges (Ganga) River: a famous holy river of India, which runs throughout the entire universe. She originates from the spiritual world, and she descended to the material world when Lord Vamanadeva kicked a hole in the top of the universe. It is recommended that one bathe in the Ganges for purification.

Gaudiya: refers to the region of Bengal and Bangladesh, used synonymously with *Gaudiya Vaishnavism*; a follower of Lord Chaitanya.

Gaudiya Vaishnava: traditionally, a *Vaishnava* born in Bengal, or, more generally and commonly, any *Vaishnava* who follows the pure teachings of Lord Chaitanya. A *Vaishnava* is a devotee of Vishnu or Krishna. Hence, a *Gaudiya Vaishnava* is a practitioner of the form of *Vaishnavism* associated with Bengal, inaugurated by Chaitanya Mahaprabhu and his followers some 500 years ago. Regardless of its earthly origins, it is an eternal system for returning to the spiritual world.

Gaura Purnima: the full moon celebration of the appearance of Shri Chaitanya Mahaprabhu, who appeared in West Bengal around 1486 of the Christian era. When he appeared to take birth, there was a full lunar eclipse, and as per custom, the Hindu population took bath in holy rivers, such as the Ganges, and sang the holy names, such as those that make up the *Hare Krishna* mantra. Shri Chaitanya used this event as a way to introduce his mission of propagating the chanting of the holy names, the primary method for God realization and developing love for Krishna.

Gaurasundara: the beautiful, golden-complexioned Lord, Shri Chaitanya Mahaprabhu.

Gopis: The cowherd girls of Vraja (Vrindavan), who are generally the counterparts of Shri Krishna's *hladini-sakti*, personified as Shrimati Radharani. They assist her as maidservants in her conjugal pastimes with the Supreme Personality of Godhead. The *gopis* are Gopala Krishna's cowherd girlfriends, who are his most surrendered and confidential devotees.

Govardhan hill: a large hill that is dear to Lord Krishna and his devotees. Krishna held it up for seven days to protect his devotees in Vrindavan from a devastating storm sent by the deva Indra.

Govardhan sila: stones from Govardhan Hill in Vrindavan. Lord Chaitanya and Raghunatha dasa Goswami inaugurated worship of these stones. On the basis of statements from *Shrimad Bhagavatam*, Lord Chaitanya established that Govardhan Hill and Krishna are non-different. By such worship, Raghunatha dasa Goswami received the direct *darshana* (audience or vision) of the Lord.

Govinda: A principle, primary name for Krishna that means, "one who gives pleasure to the land, cows, and senses."

Grihamedi: the opposite of *grihasthas*, those who live together for self-centered, materialistic, or extended selfish activities, without any endeavor for spiritual advancement. They are considered at best neglectful, and at worst envious of others. The word *medhi* indicates jealousy of others.

Grihastha(s): those who take sacred marriage vows to live together, often with children, for the purpose of serving Krishna and developing love for him. They meet their material necessities in a way that fosters spiritual cultivation.

Guru: a spiritual master; one who initiates others into spiritual life and teaches them through the *Vedic* scriptures and through his or her example. There are many types of gurus who perform various functions, such as: the *vartma-pradarshaka guru,* who first introduces one to spiritual life; the *diksha guru,* who initiates one into the tradition; the *shiksha guru,* who gives relevant instructions, and so on. While one may have a singular *diksha guru*, one may have any number of *shiksha gurus*. The *diksha* and *shiksha* manifestations are considered equal manifestations of Krishna. The decision to accept a guru is a voluntary, personal affair; it cannot be legislated by others. Krishna responds to our inner necessity for guidance, even if it is controversial to others.

Hari: one of the many names of Krishna. It has many meanings, one of which is, "one who takes everything away." This meaning causes some people to avoid worshiping Krishna for fear of losing their material possessions. However, in the spiritual realm, this is a favorite name of Krishna, which means, "he who steals our hearts." These two meanings show us the contrasting ways in which people see God.

Indra: considered the king of the heavenly realm of empowered beings (devas) entrusted to supply the necessities for all living beings. He is known for coordinating the rain, and his weapon is the thunderbolt. He corresponds in Greek mythology to Zeus.

Japa: the soft repetition of a mantra (for *Gaudiya Vaishnavas*, primarily the *Hare Krishna* mantra) on prayer beads.

Kali-yuga: the last and most degraded of a continual cycle of four ages. Considered the iron age, or the age of quarrel and hypocrisy, it began five thousand years ago and lasts a total of 432,000 years.

(Krishna) Karnamrita: a very important and spiritually advanced scripture written by Shrila Bilvamangala Thakura and found in South India by Lord Chaitanya (along with *Brahma Samhita*, which he greatly relished). Of this book, Lord Chaitanya said, "There is no comparison to the *Krishna Karnamrita* within the three worlds. By studying this book, one is elevated to the knowledge of pure devotional service to Krishna. One who constantly reads the *Krishna Karnamrita* can fully understand the beauty and melodious taste of the pastimes of Lord Krishna" (*Chaitanya Charitamrita, Madhya* 9.307-8). The author of this book is also named Karnamrita. *Karna* means ear, and *amrita* means eternal nectar, so *karnamrita* means eternal nectar for the ear.

Kirtan: glorification of the Supreme Lord; narrating or singing the glories of the Supreme Personality of Godhead and his holy names; the devotional process of chanting the names and glories of the Supreme Lord. A related Sanskrit word is *kirti* (fame). Hence, *kirtan* means to glorify for the fame of the Supreme Lord. *Sankirtan* means to glorify congregationally.

(Lord) Krishna: Gaudiya Vaishnavas consider him to be the original Supreme Personality of Godhead from whom unlimited

expansions emanate. Krishna means "all-attractive" and "irresistible." In his highest aspect, he is God fallen in love with his devotees, forgetful even of his own godhood in order to taste this loving mellow. He has little interest in being worshiped as God or in the duties we generally attribute to God; therefore, he expands himself as Lord Vishnu to manifest and maintain the infinite universes and planets within them. We could also say he is God beyond God, or he is the source of God!

Krishna consciousness: the remembrance of Krishna; living in such a way as to always remember Krishna. This expression is also used synonymously to describe the practice of Bhakti.

Liberation: freedom from the material concept of life; establishment in one's constitutional position as an eternal servant of God; in Sanskrit, *moksha* or *mukti*. *Vedic* culture guides mankind through four stages of value development: *dharma* (religiosity), *artha* (economic development), *kama* (sense gratification), and *moksha* (liberation of the soul from birth and death). Beyond even *moksha*, as taught Chaitanya Mahaprabhu, is the fifth and unsurpassed stage, love of God (*prema pumarto mahan*). It could also be loosely compared to the Christian idea of salvation.

Lila: as opposed to karma (being forced to take birth by material reactions, good or bad), *lila* denotes transcendental pastimes, activities performed by God or his devotees for a spiritual purpose, such as: to save the devotees from feeling intense separation from him, to demonstrate the activities of the spiritual world in order to attract all living beings, or to reestablish true religious principles. In general, *lila* refers to the endlessly expanding spiritual activities and pastimes of Krishna in the spiritual world.

Maha-mantra: the "great mantra" or the chant for deliverance; the recommended means (according to the *Vedas* and Lord Chaitanya) for self-realization in the current Age of Kali: *Hare Krishna, Hare Krishna, Krishna Krishna, Hare Hare / Hare Rama, Hare Rama, Rama Rama, Hare Hare.* In one sense, there is no real petition in this mantra since it is composed only of the Lord's holy names; however, Prabhupada gave the mood of this prayer when he translated its meaning as follows: "Oh Lord, energy of the Lord, please engage me in your service." To serve and love God with no material motive is the attitude of pure devotees.

Mahaprabhu: Prabhu means master, and *maha* means great, so Mahaprabhu was great or supreme even among the masters.

Maha-prasad(am): pure vegetarian sanctified food that consists of remnants from the plate offered directly to Krishna in his Deity form. The remnants of the Deity are given to the devotees. In this Bhakti philosophy (given in *Bhagavad Gita*, 9.26-27), everything we do, say, and eat should first be offered to Krishna for his pleasure. Generally, food is offered to Krishna in a special ceremony, a ritual similar to saying grace, but more formal and precise. Whatever is offered to Krishna in love and devotion is considered spiritual. In this way, by honoring Krishna's remnants, a devotee becomes purified and spiritualized. Some sects refer to any offered food as *maha-prasad(am)*.

Mala: prayer beads used for chanting mantras. Among *Gaudiya Vaishnavas,* the *mala* are generally made from sacred tulasi wood and are used in chanting *japa*, one's prescribed repetitions of the *Hare Krishna* mantra.

Mandira: a temple of God.

Mantra: sometimes translated as "mind deliverer." In *Vedic* tradition, a mantra is composed in Sanskrit and used in meditation on and worship of God. It may be chanted in *japa* or sung in *kirtan*.

Maya: illusion or "that which is not;" the energy of the Supreme Lord that deludes living entities into forgetfulness of their spiritual nature and of God; to measure, as in to attempt to calculate God or understand his divine pastimes (*lila*) by mere material reasoning.

Mayavadi: One who propounds the philosophy originally taught by the great philosopher of India, Shankar-acharya, which posits that God is featureless and impersonal, that devotion to a personal Godhead is false, that the material creation of the Lord is also false, and that the ultimate goal of life is to become existentially one with the all-pervading, impersonal Absolute.

(Lord or Shri) Nityananda (Nitai): Lord Chaitanya's associate, considered to be his brother, who is also an incarnation of God or Shri Balarama. He is often rather unconventional in his activities as he is overwhelmed with spiritual ecstasy. Thus, he is called *avadhuta*. which means mad, or unconventional, saint. He is extremely merciful in giving out *Krishna prema*, love for Krishna. The spiritual master is said to represent Nityananda,

since like Nityananda, he gives Krishna consciousness to whomever he meets, regardless of their disqualifications.

Paramahamsa: a topmost, God-realized, swanlike devotee of the Supreme Lord; the highest stage of *sannyasa*.

Paramatma: the Supersoul (Oversoul), or God as in in-dwelling Witness and Permitter; the localized aspect of Vishnu, or the expansion of the Supreme Lord residing in the heart of each embodied living entity and pervading all material nature.

Prasadam (prasad): see *maha-prasad*.

Prabhu: master; used as an address to another devotee of Krishna. In other words, it is meant to be a title of respect to another, and it is intended to evoke humility about one's own position.

Prabhupada: see Shrila Prabhupada.

Radha (Radharani): Lord Krishna's most intimate consort; the personification of the internal pleasure potency of Lord Krishna. She appeared in this world as the daughter of King Vrishabhanu and Kirti-devi, and she is the Queen of Vrindavan. As the most favorite consort of Krishna in Vrindavan, she is situated at Lord Krishna's left on altars and in pictures. She is the feminine counterpart of Lord Krishna. She directs the *ananda* potency (*hladini-shakti*) for the transcendental pleasure of the Lord.

Rasa: There is no English equivalent; however, we attempt to describe *rasa* as the experience of a relationship between the

Lord and the living entities, or the mellow (sweet taste) of such a relationship. There are five principal varieties of *rasa*: 1) a neutral relationship (*shanta rasa*), appreciation of God's greatness without service; 2) a relationship as a servant (*dasya rasa*); 3) a relationship as a friend (*sakhya rasa*); 4) a relationship in the mood of a parent (*vatsalya rasa*); and 5) a relationship as a conjugal lover (*madhurya rasa*). *Madhurya rasa* is objectively considered the highest due the degree of selflessness and giving implicit in the relationship. Of course, whatever *rasa* one has with Krishna is perfect and totally satisfying. Just as our present material body permits us to engage in karma (physical activities), so the spiritual *rasa* body permits us to engage in *lila* (Krishna's endlessly expanding spiritual activities).

Sadhana: "the means" for spiritual awakening, such as: hearing and chanting the holy names of Krishna, Rama, and Govinda; hearing devotional scriptures; hearing great saints speak from the scriptures; serving the Deity; worshiping Tulasi; and serving *Vaishnavas*. *Sadhana* entails learning and practicing the rules and regulations of spiritual discipline, the dos and don'ts of spiritual life. While the rules themselves other that pure devotion and chanting the holy name don't deliver love of God, they help regulate one's life and create a favorable mental and physical environment essential for spiritual life in Bhakti Yoga.

Sadhya: "the goal" of *Gaudiya Vaishnavas*: *Krishna prema*, love for Krishna.

Sankirtana: San means group, and *kirtan* means to glorify. Thus, *sankirtan* means to glorify congregationally the fame of the Supreme Lord by chanting his holy names. *Sankirtan* is the *yuga-dharma*, the main occupation and attribute of the present age (*Kali-yuga*). It was introduced by this age's incarnation of God, Shri Chaitanya Mahaprabhu, who taught *sankirtan* by his life's example.

Sankirtan yajna: the sacrifice prescribed for the Age of Kali, namely, congregational chanting of the name, fame, and pastimes of the Supreme Personality of Godhead.

Shakti: the energies or potencies of God variously manifested. For example, in the *Vedas,* God is often compared both to the sun itself and to the sun's powers of heat and light by which it sustains the universe.

Shastra: the revealed scriptures obeyed by all those who follow the *Vedic* teachings. *Shas* means "to regulate and direct" and *tra* means "an instrument." Shastra refers to *Vedic* literature or the *Vedic* scriptures—one of the three authorities for a *Vaishnava*.

Shrila Prabhupada: a formal, though affectionate title given to His Divine Grace A. C. Bhaktivedanta Swami Prabhupada, the founder-acharya of the International Society for Krishna Consciousness (ISKCON), or the Hare Krishna Movement. He came from India in 1965 on the order of his guru to spread the teachings of Lord Chaitanya and to promote the chanting of the *Hare Krishna maha-mantra*. It is thought that he was specially empowered to spread these teachings all over the world, paving the way for many other preachers to follow the path he blazed. His own guru also had the title of Prabhupada, which means, "at whose feet many masters sit."

Shrimad Bhagavatam: also known as the *Bhagavat Purana*, considered by *Gaudiya Vaishnavas* to be the emperor of all scriptures. It is the commentary on the *Vedanta Sutra*. The *Bhagavatam* contains the essence of *Vedic* thought, and it was written by the author of all the *Vedas*, Shrila Vyasadeva, in his spiritual maturity. It was the favorite scripture of Lord Chaitanya, as it teaches the highest standard of devotion to Krishna and describes how to understand the relationship between Krishna, the soul, his devotees, and the material world. It also gives the general principles and philosophies of Bhakti. It recounts many of Krishna's important incarnations, as well as his personal pastimes that took place when he appeared on this planet five thousand years ago. These narrations give us a sample of the activities of the spiritual world.

Tulasi, Tulasidevi, or Vrinda, Vrindadevi: a great devotee of Krishna who appears in various forms as an eternal associate of the Lord, as a maidservant, and as a special plant used in worship. Devotees of Krishna wear neck beads and chant on *japa* beads made from her wood, symbolizing the desire to receive her favor in pleasing Krishna. When we offer food to Krishna, we place a Tulasi leaf on each preparation. We only approach Krishna by the mercy of his devotees, and Tulasi is one of the foremost. Krishna's home is also named after her: Vrindavan, or the forest of Tulasi.

Vaishnava: in a liberal sense, anyone who accepts the supremacy of God and endeavors to serve him; in a specific sense, a devotee (one who is devoted to Vishnu or Krishna and follows the teachings of the *Vedic* scriptures). A *Gaudiya Vaishnava* is a disciple in the succession of gurus from Lord Chaitanya Mahaprabhu.

Vedas: the original revealed scriptures that appeared in India. They are considered eternal, like the Supreme Lord, and appeared by revelation to realized sages. Before modern history, they were passed down through oral tradition. Shrila Vyasadeva compiled all the branches of *Vedic* knowledge and wrote them down for the people of the current Age of Kali. In this age, the *Vedas* are difficult to understand or even study, so the epic histories and *Puranas*, especially *Shrimad Bhagavatam*, are more essential for gaining access to the teachings of the *Vedas* than the original four *Vedas*.

Vedic: pertaining to the spiritual standards and moral codes of the *Vedas*; more broadly, an adjective to describe one who follows *Vedic* authority; that which is derived from *Vedic* authority.

(Lord) Vishnu: the Supreme Personality of Godhead in his four-armed expansion in Vaikuntha, or the majestic part of God's kingdom in super royal opulence, where he is worshipped on awe and reverence; a plenary expansion of the original Supreme Personality of Godhead, Shri Krishna. Vishnu enters into the material universe before creation and supervises the maintenance of the created universe.

Vyasadeva: also known as Veda Vyasa, he is considered to be the literary incarnation of God who compiled all the *Vedic* scriptures into written form (which before that time were maintained by oral tradition) for the forgetful people of the present Age of Kali.

Epilogue

I have rushed to publish this first of two volumes of my collected free verse poems in the middle of dealing with a cancer diagnosis and adopting complimentary protocols that give me the best chance to survive and thrive. I would have liked to adapt this book for a broader audience, but time is of the essence. Studying what cancer actually is and the politics around conventional treatment has been mind-blowing. Big money, greed, and self-interest spoil everything—education, healthcare, medicine, news media, sports, business, and government. Although I don't feel it is my time to leave the world, I know that is a possibility. As a result, time and my life in general have taken on a new urgency.

I am attempting to accomplish goals I have been putting off. However long I may live, I feel I have a new lease on life. My poems document my life. In this spirit, I haven't deleted those I might have removed under normal circumstances (are there really any?). This and my second collection of poems are important to me as an embodiment of my life and the lessons I've learned. I like them all, even though some are much better to me than others. I love the feelings I have put into them.

There is no tomorrow; cancer will kill or save me: These are the thoughts that came to me this morning. It's sobering, but I'm forever hopeful with positive expectancy. There is no meaning to seeing my shortcomings and life issues unless I am willing to do something about them. Spiritual life is meant for thinking deeply and creating habits and practices that are favorable for spiritual advancement (for me, that means progress in Bhakti Yoga). Practically everyone who is engaged in spiritual cultivation has to, or has had to, overcome lethargy and the tendency to be comfortable with mediocrity and complacency. It seems easier to stay the same and do the familiar, even if we are only going around in a circle, making no forward motion. We have to realize that there is no bright future in that—just more of where we are now.

Only by doing the difficult work of uprooting our *anarthas* (unwanted habits of thinking and acting) through introspection, prayer, and spiritual practice can we realize our true happiness and the means for lasting fulfillment. Those of us who have been on a spiritual journey for a long time may find that our initial enthusiasm was greater than it is today.

During my existential crisis at age 18, I was desperate to find meaning and escape my intense suffering. I was immature and naïve in both material and spiritual understanding, and yet I was sincere. As time marched on, I had to deal with my life issues and make peace with my upbringing, and thus, I couldn't sustain the level of my youthful commitment and focus. However, my emotional inner work and my initial urgency and sincerity bore fruit by helping me remain engaged in the basics of my spiritual practice. These practices, along with many years of intense prayer for help and spiritual advancement have continued to sustain me through my current health challenge, which is pushing me upward. True sincerity is invincible even when we stumble—such is the Lord's mercy.

Remembering the days of my youthful enthusiasm has reminded me that while external surrender—giving up possessions, jobs, and the like for the pursuit of transcendence—can be valuable in youth, it's much easier than examining and purging bad habits and realizing our ineligibility for Bhakti. This comes with the maturity that arises out of years of spiritual practice and life experience.

At least I can say for myself, even though I lost the intensity of my original spiritual search and spent too many years as a casual Bhakti practitioner, my spiritual vigor is being rekindled. I am praying that my current situation can make my spiritual fire blaze, and that I can share the wealth of my enthused spiritual practice with whomever I encounter. My motto: everything that happens in my life is meant for my highest spiritual good.

There is no tomorrow.
Surrender must be now.
Acknowledging my disqualifications—
laziness and material distractions—
I refuse to let them define me.
My excuses are all lame,
without any currency or meaning.
I can only pray for mercy and sincerity,
which supersedes everything.
I must empty myself today
of the unessential and superficial.

The world is a perilous mess.
All I can do is offer my soul,

fulfill my need for power
by connecting to our Source,
which gives its illumination and love,
full of spiritual nourishment.
I offer myself so I can give what is required
to share God's love and kindness.
I can show a way to wholeness,
the divine potential of everyone,
a way to fulfill our hankering heart
by using our nature and karma
as an instrument of divine love—
for me, the greatest blessing!

ABOUT THE ARTIST: NOEL PARENTI

Noel Parenti (Shyamlal Das) is a Bhakti yogi who has studied many forms and styles of yoga. He received his teacher training in Ananda Yoga at The Expanding Light in California. Formerly a dancer, actor, choreographer, and teacher of tap, theater dance, mime, and movement for actors, Noel's background in the performing arts includes stage, film, television, and commercial work. While on tour with the musical, *Crazy For You*, he passed his leisure hours sketching with crayons. Eventually, he found his way with form, color, and composition working with watercolors, acrylics, and pen and ink. His subject matter is primarily spiritual, centered on Krishna. The front and back cover—the meditating yogi and Krishna's "lotus" foot, respectively—and all the line drawings within this book are from his collected works. He and his wife live in Winston-Salem and teach yoga. He can be reached at noel@newplanetyoga.com.

ABOUT THE AUTHOR: KARNAMRITA DAS

I was born on June 22, 1950 in Los Angeles, California with the name Christopher John Cox. In 1954, we moved to San Francisco, where I completed all my schooling. My life as a child, though certainly a mixed experience, was often painful, confusing, and ultimately unsatisfying. Mine was a violent, alcoholic family, and my mom and I tried our best to survive my father's rage.

All in all, my early life proved to be a catalyst that impelled me to search out alternatives to the materialistic status quo of the time and continue the unfinished spiritual development of my previous lives. Although not a spiritual family, it turned out to be a favorable environment for a spiritual quest, mixed with the hippie counter-culture movement of the late 1960's. After a year of college, an existential crisis prompted me to begin a full-time search for the meaning of life. I became a vegetarian and frequently spent time in Muir Woods, a redwood forest in Marin County, California, studying the cycles of nature and books from various spiritual traditions. Those days were punctuated with mystical experiences.

I concluded that I needed to become a monk in some tradition in order to immerse myself in spirituality. After studying many religious and spiritual paths, I came in contact with the books and disciples of *Shrila A. C. Bhaktivedanta Swami Prabhupada*, and I began visiting a Krishna temple (ISKCON) in Berkeley, California. Soon, I experienced that this tradition spoke deeply to my soul. It felt like home, and I became a *brahmachari*, or monk, receiving *diksha* in 1970. I was given the name, Karnamrita das (a servant of the sound-nectar of immortality, or Krishna *lila*) to symbolize a "second birth" into spirituality.

For the first three years as a novice monk, I primarily studied and distributed my guru's books. Gradually, I became involved in temple services or *puja* (Deity worship), becoming a head cook and *pujari* (temple priest). I continued this service for the next eleven years at various centers in America, Asia, India, and Australia. The realizations, feelings, and opportunities for service I derived from worshipping Krishna in his many Deity forms have provided me with a deep foundation for my continued spiritual development, enabling me to function in many different cultural and social arenas.

Trained in many energy-healing and alternative health modalities, such as Reiki, hypnotherapy, Emotional Release Therapy, and healing prayer, I incorporate healing into my life, work, and service. I serve with my wife, Archana Siddhi dasi, an LCSW, on the *Grihastha* Vision Team, facilitating workshops and working with couples in therapy and premarital education. We've been living an idyllic life for the last twelve years on four acres of land in rural North Carolina, serving our Deities, focusing on our spiritual practices, working with couples, and writing. I compiled 90 entries from my blog on Krishna.com into a book, the title of which—*Give to Live*—is a code for how I endeavor to live, love, and serve. The volume of collected poems you are reading was published at warp speed, propelled by my current health crisis.

In November of 2015, I was diagnosed with stage 3 nasopharyngeal cancer, which changed my life radically. Embarking on a study of cancer and alternative treatments, I altered my diet accordingly and adopted many protocols to strengthen my immune system and fight cancer. I traveled to a cancer clinic in Mexico for further treatment which is ongoing. Most importantly, I realized that to fulfill my life's purpose I need to write and speak more. Thus, I'm currently on a speaking tour to share my realizations about various spiritual and personal growth topics. My primary theme is, "How Facing Death Can Help One Live More Fully Today."

You can read my blogs on Krishna.com:
www.Krishna.com/blogs/karnamritadas,
or on Facebook:
www.facebook.com/karnamrita.das.
Or, you can contact me via email:
karnamrita@yahoo.com.

Prayer

In the next installment in my series of free verse poems, I have an entire chapter on prayer and japa (the soft chanting of the maha-mantra), but under the circumstances, I may not have another opportunity to publish. Thus, I wanted to share my favorite poem on prayer, since prayer is my main spiritual support and constant companion.

Prayer Is Life

Prayer is my life;
it always sustains me
through the day and night,
in pain or joy,
setbacks or successes.
I go to bed with prayer;
awakening, I bow down,
remembering my gurus
in gratitude for service,
amazed at my good fortune.

I pray to offer my day
to beautiful, flower-clad, Krishna,
folding my bedding with prayer,
drinking prasad (blessed) water.

My necessities are all provided,
and thus my body endures.
My soul begins to flourish—
each breath, heartbeat, and step
continues only by mercy,
Everything is his grace and kindness.

Prayer reminds me:
I'm always a servant,
a tiny, covered, spiritual spark.
But my ego inflates my smugness.
Forgetful of God for eons,
and still I'm proud
of my feeble, religious attempt
at waking and rising up.
When selfishness rules me,
I return to the holy name.

By prayer I remember Krishna,
chanting and hearing his glories.
Though stubborn, I'm still blessed
in spite of myself. When I call out,
kind and generous Krishna smiles
as I share my life with him.
I'm saved even by poor prayers,
making thousands of attempts—
some with heart, other officially
acknowledging Krishna's love.

Daily intensified prayer
before Radha-Krishna Deities—

the core of my life:
I sit before them,
petitioning through *Hare Krishna,*
praying to be emptied out,
freed from sensual demands,
ignorance, illusion, and forgetfulness.
Waking up to my true nature,
I cheer others to stay the course.

Lord, please accept me—
more, let me accept you—
fully, completely, absolutely,
here and now, now and forever.
Let offence—past, present, or future—
or whatever hinders my progress
toward taking full shelter of you
in loving service, let that be finished,
replaced by the constant serving mood:
pure devotion, my only food.

I'm Krishna's eternal part,
serving him and all beings,
giving myself by love's power,
yet aspiring for humility like grass
and tolerance like the trees.
Giving respect, not wanting it,
I know I'm always dependent
on his grace and facility.
By prayer, I'm aware of
my shortcoming, and my spiritual goal.

A glimpse of his mercy is revealed
as I plead to chant purely,
hearing one mantra at a time
until I'm totally, unconditionally his.
By living, feeling, and acting in surrender,
becoming one with Bhakti in love,
every day I move closer by prayer
to the blue cowherd, Krishna,
the love and sustainer of my life,
a lasting friend like no other!

Facing Death to Live More Fully

I want to include this, as it's my current life focus:

*We need to be reminded that there is nothing
morbid about honestly confronting the fact of life's end,
and preparing for it so that we may go gracefully and
peacefully. The fact is, that we cannot truly face life
until we have learned to face the fact that i
t will be taken away from us.*
Rev. Billy Graham

*We do not know whether it is good to live or die. Therefore, we
should not take delight in living nor should we tremble at the
thought of death. We should be equiminded toward both.
This is the ideal.*
Gandhi

*The only religious way to think of death is as part and parcel of life;
to regard it, with the understanding and the emotions,
as the inviolable condition of life.*
Thomas Mann

*Death is the only immortal who treats us all alike, whose pity and
whose peace and whose refuge are for all—the soiled and the pure,*

the rich and the poor, the loved and the unloved.
Mark Twain, on his deathbed

Death is, to us here, the most terrible word we know. But when we have tasted its reality, it will mean to us birth, deliverance, a new creation of ourselves.
George Merriman

Live as if you were to die tomorrow.
Learn as if you were to live forever.
Mahatma *Gandhi*

As a person puts on new garments, giving up old ones, the soul similarly accepts new material bodies, giving up the old and useless ones.
Bhagavad Gita, 2.22

Don't think this won't happen to you.
My guru, Shrila Prabhupada, weak and bedridden in his last days—he frequently taught that our Bhakti will be tested at the time of death.

Philosophy is preparation for death and dying.
Socrates

I Am Dying! Why Is There Death?

This is an excerpt from my book, *Give to Live*, which has a whole chapter on death and dying. This creative dialog was inspired by a famous health enthusiast who had untreatable (by modern methods at least) cancer. She couldn't believe she had this disease since she lived such a healthy lifestyle. For similar reasons, some of my friends were surprised that my body developed cancer, or they were surprised because they thought I was spiritually advanced. Disease happens, as does old age and death, to every embodied soul.

We may live relatively better and suffer less, but misery comes to us all. Spiritual advancement helps us deal with pain and aging, but not escape its appearance. Great souls teach us how to live with disease, old age, death, and dying, while reminding us, as does scripture, that although the body inevitably declines, our soul is eternal. Life's purpose is to realize our eternal nature as consciousness and as part of God.

I am dying!
Are you sad?
Or glad????
I'm mad #@$%$#&^!!
Why me?
Why is God doing this to me? Of all people!

Come on, really!!!
After all, I am a good person—not perfect mind you—but compared to those really bad people harming and killing others, or ruining the environment, I *am* a good person.
I deserve a little credit, you know?
And why are so many bad people doing so well?? Meanwhile, I'm condemned!
Terrible!
Horrible! (No, not *Haribol*!)
Listen: I help others in need, give in charity.
I have been a vegetarian for twenty years. I eat only organic, locally produced food, I ride a bike to work, and for God's sake, I have been recycling since before it was cool and encouraged.
And I exercise regularly, I am—or thought I was—in really good shape. I have the perfect fat to muscle ratio. I am very conscious of my impact on the planet and my relationship to others.
I was happy and good and peaceful and I didn't get into trouble. But now, this cancer.
The doc says its terminal.
This just can't be. I am doing everything better than right.
Totally unexpected!
I just can't believe it is happening to me of all people.
I still have so many plans I want to complete. If only I could have a little more time to finish them. So many people would benefit!
Not fair or good! @#$%&%@!
God is really making a big mistake!! That is for sure!

No, this is not my personal story—yet. But it could be mine, or yours. If we are advanced in spiritual consciousness, we will be able to meet our death in a more peaceful way than the above account! We all will face the death of the body eventually. It may come without notice, or at the worst possible time from the material perspective.

A number of wise persons have said in various ways that in order to really live, we have to deal with the fact of death. Not everyone is afraid of death, has a death phobia, or tries to never think of it (like my Mom). Still, we need to be educated about death, as well as about the nature of the world and our place in it. And while we are here, we need to know how to really live and for what purpose!

My guru, Shrila Prabhupada, said that one of the facilities of human life (which many are not using today) is metaphysical or spiritual inquiry, the ability to ask such essential questions as: *Who am I? Is there a God, and if so, what is my relationship to him/her/it? Why do we suffer and experience pain? Why is there evil if God is all good? What is the purpose of life and death?*

Cancer Brings the Seeds of Change

Sitting in the sun room,
observing the dancing trees
swaying in the strong wind,
watching unlimited seeds fall
like snowflakes in a storm,
I contemplate the lessons
symbolized by the cycles of nature:
decay, death, and rebirth.
Nature's perfect intelligence
instructs and feeds us,
preparing for future generations,
all sustained by God's laws.

Driving to morning services,
a thick fog blankets the road.
Backing out of the driveway
down the foggy, wet, muddy road,
my wife comments she couldn't imagine
driving in this condition.
Reflecting on this, I remember
an appropriate Bible verse:
We walk by faith, not by sight.
I think of this in relation to my life
and my cancer diagnosis.

Cancer is an "obvious" push
to change, yet I still have to choose
to feel cursed or blessed,
to see cancer as grace,

the Lord's kind embrace.
Still, it is certain that now
the present has more value,
a special opening to grow,
an urgency for divine shelter.
It's a push and test of my spiritual life,
calling me to prepare and strengthen
my faith, forcing me to ask honestly:
what have I realized,
and what shall I do?

I look within and forward
instead of to the past
where old desires lurk
and beckon me to follow,
where the past invites me
to relish the old cycle
of enjoyment and renunciation.
Chewing the chewed repeatedly,
it's that bad rerun yet again—
how many times have I failed?
But no matter; it's a new day.
I remember the soul is "me;"
I'm not the temporary body.
True joy and peace
aren't found in the world.
I must decide what is true
and then, what I must do.

We show what's important
by our actions and our absorption.

But, when the guillotine rises,
a new burden is created—
distress and fear, or opportunity.
During the waiting game,
all outcomes are possible.
Dealing with uncertainty,
I awaken and reevaluate,
wondering if I am ready
to happily embrace death
with no regrets or hesitations,
knowing I did my best,
joyfully walking through
one door to enter another,
or staying here with increased
faith, conviction, and wisdom.

*Go within
Or
go without!*

www.ingramcontent.com/pod-product-compliance
Lightning Source LLC
LaVergne TN
LVHW011152080426
835508LV00007B/359